# Hutchinson GCSE Computer Studies Factfinder

First published 1992

Copyright © Helicon Publishing 1992

All rights reserved

Helicon Publishing Ltd
20 Vauxhall Bridge Road
London SW1V 2SA

Random House Australia (Pty) Ltd
20 Alfred Street, Milsons Point
Sydney 2061, Australia

Random House New Zealand Ltd
18 Poland Road, Glenfield
Auckland 10, New Zealand

Random House South Africa (Pty) Ltd
PO Box 337, Bergvlei 2012
South Africa

Set in Century Schoolbook

Phototypeset by Intype, London

ISBN 0 09 177153 6

Printed and bound in Great Britain
by Cox & Wyman Ltd, Reading, Berkshire

**Consultant Editor**
Mark Bindley

**Project Editor**
Roger Watson

**Coordinating Editor**
Sara Jenkins-Jones

**Text Editors**
Ingrid von Essen
Jonathan Wainwright

**Design**
Ken Brooks Design Services

The front cover includes a picture of English mathematician
Charles Babbage, who devised the forerunners of the computer.

**absolute** (of a value) real and unchanging. For example, an *absolute address* is a location in memory and an *absolute cell reference* is a single fixed cell in a spreadsheet display. The opposite of absolute is ▷relative.

**access** the way in which ▷file access is provided so that the data can be stored, retrieved, or updated by the computer.

**access time** or *reaction time* the time taken by a computer, after an instruction has been given, to read from or write to ▷memory.

**accumulator** special register, or memory location, situated in the ▷arithmetic and logic unit of the computer processor. It is used to hold the result of a calculation temporarily or to store data that are being transferred.

**acoustic coupler** device that enables computer data to be transmitted and received through a normal telephone handset; the handset rests on the coupler to make the connection. A small speaker within the device is used to convert the computer's digital output data into sound signals, which are then picked up by the handset and transmitted through the telephone system. At the receiving telephone, a second acoustic coupler converts the sound signals back into digital data for input into a computer.

Unlike a ▷modem, an acoustic coupler does not require direct connection to the telephone system. However, interference from background noise means that the quality of transmission is poorer than with a modem, and more errors are likely to arise.

**acronym** word formed from the initial letters and/or syllables of other words, intended as a pronounceable abbreviation—for

*acoustic coupler*

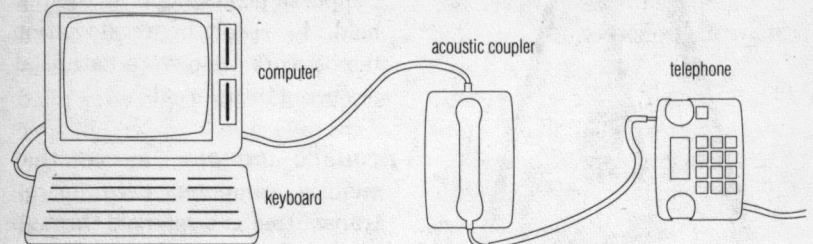

example, RAM (*r*andom-*a*ccess *m*emory) and FORTRAN (*for*mula *tran*slation). In contrast, the initial letters making up an abbreviation are each pronounced separately—for example, ALU (*a*rithmetic and *l*ogic *u*nit).

**ADA** high-level programming language, developed and owned by the US Department of Defense, designed for use in situations in which a computer directly controls a process or machine, such as a military aircraft. The language took more than five years to specify, and became commercially available only in the late 1980s. It is named after the English mathematician Ada Augusta Byron (1815–1851).

**ADC** abbreviation for ◊*analogue-to-digital converter*.

**adder** electronic circuit in a computer that carries out the process of adding two binary numbers. A separate adder is needed for each pair of binary ◊bits to be added. Such circuits are essential components of a computer's ◊arithmetic and logic unit (ALU).

**address** number indicating a specific location in a computer memory. At each address, a single piece of data can be stored. For microcomputers, this normally amounts to one ◊byte (enough to represent a single character).

The maximum capacity of a computer memory depends on how many memory addresses it can have. This is normally measured in units of 1,024 bytes (known as kilobytes, or K).

**address bus** the electrical pathway or ◊bus used to select the route for any particular data item as it is moved from one part of a computer to another.

**ALGOL** (acronym for *algo*rithmic *l*anguage) an early high-level programming language, developed in the 1950s and 1960s for scientific applications. A general-purpose language, ALGOL is best suited to mathematical work and has an algebraic style. Although no longer in common use, it has greatly influenced more recent languages, such as ADA and PASCAL.

**algorithm** procedure or series of steps that can be used to solve a problem. In computer science, it describes the logical sequence of operations to be performed by a program.

A ◊flow chart is a visual representation of an algorithm.

**alphanumeric data** data made up of any of the letters of the alphabet and any digit from 0 to 9. The classification of data according to the type or types of character contained enables computer ◊validation systems to check the accuracy of data: a computer can be programmed to reject entries that contain the wrong type of character. For example, a person's name would be rejected if it contained any numeric data, and a bank-account number would be rejected if it contained any alphabetic data. A car's registration number, by comparison, would be allowed to contain both alphabetic and numeric data.

**ALU** abbreviation for ◊*arithmetic and logic unit*.

**analogue** (of a quantity or device) changing continuously; by contrast a ◊digital quantity or device varies in series of distinct steps. For example, an analogue clock measures time by means of a continuous movement of hands around a dial, whereas a digital clock measures time with a numerical display that changes in a series of discrete steps.

Most computers are digital devices. Therefore, any signals and data from an analogue device must be passed through a suitable ◊analogue-to-digital converter before they can be received and processed by computer. Similarly, output signals from digital computers must be passed through a digital-to-analogue converter

# analogue computer

*analogue-to-digital converter*

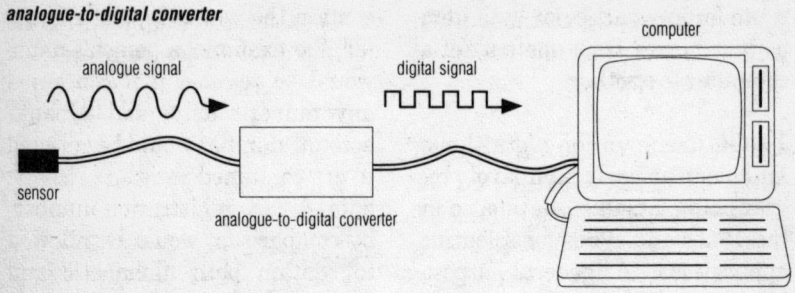

before they can be received by an analogue device.

**analogue computer** computer designed to receive and process continuously varying (analogue) data. Analogue computers are rarer than digital computers, and are often special-purpose machines built to monitor and control other devices.

**analogue-to-digital converter** (ADC) electronic circuit that converts an analogue signal into a digital one. Such a circuit is needed to convert the signal from an analogue device into a digital signal for input into a computer. For example, many ◊sensors designed to measure physical quantities, such as temperature and pressure, produce an analogue voltage signal and this must be passed through an ADC before computer input and processing. A ◊digital-to-analogue converter performs the opposite process.

**analyst** person who carries out ◊systems analysis. An analyst prepares a report on an existing data processing system and makes proposals for changes and improvements. See also ◊computer personnel.

**AND gate** in electronics, a type of ◊logic gate.

**applications package** the set of programs and related documentation (such as instruction manuals) used in a particular application. For example, a typical payroll applications package would consist of separate programs for the entry of data, updating the master files, and printing the pay slips, plus documentation in the form of program details and instructions for use.

**applications program** program designed to carry out a task for the benefit of the computer user — for example, calculating pay slips or word processing. In contrast, a ◊systems program carries out tasks related to the operation and performance of the computer itself, for example, organizing backing stage.

**argument** the value on which a ◊function operates. For example, if the argument 16 is operated on by the function 'square root', the answer 4 is produced.

**arithmetic and logic unit** (ALU) the part of the ◊central processing unit (CPU) that performs the basic arithmetic and logic operations on data.

**array** in programming, a list of values that can all be referred to by a single ◊variable name. Separate values within the array are distinguished by using a ***subscript*** alongside the variable name.

Consider, for example, this list of highest daily temperatures:

|  | *temperature (°C)* |
|---|---|
| *day* 1 | 22 |
| *day* 2 | 23 |
| *day* 3 | 19 |
| *day* 4 | 21 |

This array might be stored with the single variable name 'temp'. Separate elements of the array would then be identified with subscripts. So, for example, the array element 'temp(1)' would store the value '22', and the element 'temp(3)' would store the value '19'.

An array may use more than one subscript. For example, consider this list showing the number of pints of milk delivered to four houses:

|  | *house 1* | *house 2* | *house 3* | *house 4* |
|---|---|---|---|---|
| *day* 1 | 2 | 2 | 3 | 1 |
| *day* 2 | 2 | 1 | 2 | 1 |
| *day* 3 | 3 | 2 | 0 | 1 |
| *day* 4 | 2 | 1 | 2 | 1 |
| *day* 5 | 4 | 1 | 2 | 2 |
| *day* 6 | 4 | 5 | 4 | 4 |

If the array were given the variable name 'pint', its elements would be identified with two subscripts: one for the house and one for the day of the week. So, for example, the array element 'pint(2, 6)' would store the value '5', and the array element 'pint 3, 3)' would store the value '0'.

Arrays are useful because they allow programmers to write general routines that can process long lists of data. For example, if every price stored in an accounting program used a different variable name, separate program instructions would be needed to process each price. However, if all the prices were stored in an array, a general routine could be written to process, say, 'price($J$)', and, by allowing $J$ to take different values, could then process any individual price.

**artificial intelligence** (AI) branch of science concerned with creating computer programs that can perform actions comparable with those of an intelligent human. Current AI research covers such areas as planning (for robot behaviour), language understanding, pattern recognition, and knowledge representation.

Early AI programs, developed in the 1960s, attempted simulations of human intelligence or were aimed at general problem-solving techniques. It is currently thought that intelligent behaviour depends as much on the knowledge a system possesses as on its reasoning power. Present emphasis is on ◊knowledge-based systems, such as ◊expert systems.

**ASCII** (acronym for American standard code for information interchange) coding system in which numbers are assigned to letters, digits, and punctuation symbols. Although computers work in ◊binary number code, ASCII numbers are usually quoted as decimal or ◊hexadecimal numbers. For example, the decimal number 45 (binary 0101101) represents a hyphen, and 65 (binary 1000001) a capital A. The first 32 codes are used for control functions, such as carriage return and backspace.

Strictly speaking, ASCII is a seven-bit binary code, allowing 128 different characters to be represented, but an eighth bit is usually employed to provide ◊parity or to allow for extra characters. The system is widely used for text storage and for transmission of data between computers.

| character | binary code |
|---|---|
| A | 1000001 |
| B | 1000010 |
| C | 1000011 |
| D | 1000100 |
| E | 1000101 |
| F | 1000110 |
| G | 1000111 |
| H | 1001000 |
| I | 1001001 |
| J | 1001010 |
| K | 1001011 |
| L | 1001100 |
| M | 1001101 |
| N | 1001110 |
| O | 1001111 |
| P | 1010000 |
| Q | 1010001 |
| R | 1010010 |
| S | 1010011 |
| T | 1010100 |
| U | 1010101 |
| V | 1010110 |
| W | 1010111 |
| X | 1011000 |
| Y | 1011001 |
| Z | 1011010 |

**assembler** program that translates a program written in an assembly language into a complete ◊machine-code program that can be obeyed by a computer. Each instruction in the assembly language is translated into only one machine-code instruction.

**assembly language** low-level programming language closely related to a computer's own ◊machine code. An assembly language uses a short sequence of letters (mnemonic) to represent each machine-code instruction, and a symbol to represent each memory location. For example, the mnemonic 'HLT' might be used for 'stop' (**halt**). The programmer does not have to use the sequences of binary digits (bits) making up machine codes and addresses, and can therefore write programs more quickly and with fewer errors. Before a program in assembly language can be run by a computer, it must be translated to machine code by an assembler program.

Because they are much easier to use, high-level languages are normally used in preference to assembly languages. An assembly language may still be used in some cases, however, particularly when no suitable high-level language exists or where a very efficient ◊machine-code program is required.

**backing storage** ◊memory outside the ◊central processing unit used to store programs and data that are not in current use. Backing storage must be non-volatile memory; that is, its contents must not be lost when the power supply to the computer system is disconnected.

**backup system** duplicate computer system that can take over the operation of a main computer system in the event of an equipment failure. A large interactive system, such as an airline's ticket-booking system, cannot be out of action for even a few hours without causing considerable disruption. In such cases a complete duplicate computer system may be provided to take over and run the system should the main computer develop a fault or need maintenance. Backup systems include *incremental backup* and *full backup*.

**bar code** pattern of bars and spaces that can be read by a computer. Bar codes are widely used in retailing, industrial distribution, and public libraries. The code is read by a scanning device; the computer determines the code from the widths of the bars and the spaces.

**BASIC** (acronym for *b*eginner's *a*ll-purpose *s*ymbolic *i*nstruction *c*ode) high-level programming

*bar code*

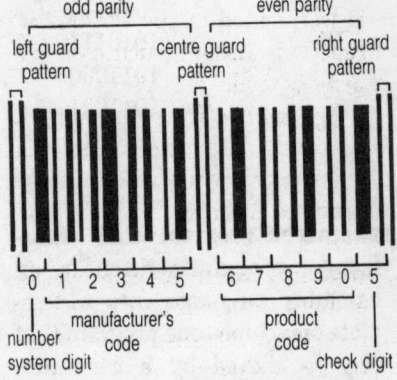

language, developed 1964, originally designed to take advantage of ◊multiuser systems (which can be used by many people at the same time). The language is relatively easy to learn and is popular among microcomputer users.

Most versions make use of an ◊interpreter, which translates BASIC into ◊machine code and allows programs to be entered and run with no intermediate translation. Some more recent versions of BASIC allow a ◊compiler to be used for this process.

**batch processing** system for processing data with little or no operator intervention. Batches of data are prepared in advance to be processed during regular 'runs' (for example, each night). This allows efficient use of the computer and is well suited to applications of a repetitive nature, such as a company payroll.

In ◊*interactive computing*, by contrast, data and instructions are entered while the processing program is running.

**baud** unit that measures the speed of data transmission. One baud represents a transmission rate of one bit per second.

**benchmark** measure of the performance of a piece of equipment or software, usually consisting of a standard program or suite of programs.

Benchmarks can indicate whether a computer is powerful enough to perform a particular task, and so enable machines to be compared. However, they provide only a very rough guide to practical performance, and may lead manufacturers to design systems that get high scores with the artificial benchmark programs but do not necessarily perform well with day-to-day programs or data.

**binary number code** code based on the binary number system, used to represent instructions and data in all modern digital computers—for example, in the ◊ASCII code system used by most microcomputers, the capital letter A is represented by the binary number 01000001.

*binary number code*

| *data* | A |
|---|---|
| *binary code* | 0 1 0 0 0 0 0 1 |
| *digital signal in the computer* | 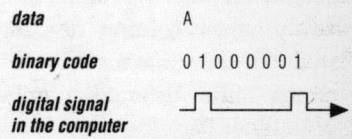 |

Because binary numbers use only the digits 0 and 1, they can be represented by any device that can exist in two different states. In a digital computer various two-state devices are used to store or transmit binary number codes—for example, circuits, which may or may not carry a voltage; discs or tapes, parts of which may or may not be magnetized; and switches, which may be open or closed.

Digital computers are designed in this way for two reasons. Firstly, it is much easier and cheaper to construct two-state devices than devices that can exist in more than two states. Secondly, communication between two-state devices is very reliable because only two different signals, 0 or 1 (on or off), need to be recognized.

**binary number system** number system to the base two, used in computing and electronics. All binary numbers are written using a combination of the digits 0 and 1. Normal decimal, or base-ten, numbers may be considered to be written under column headings based on the number ten. For example, the decimal number 2,567 stands for:

| *1,000s* | *100s* | *10s* | *1s* |
|---|---|---|---|
| *($10^3$)* | *($10^2$)* | *($10^1$)* | *($10^0$)* |
| 2 | 5 | 6 | 7 |

Binary, or base-two, numbers may be considered to be written under column headings based on the number two. For example, the binary number 1101 stands for:

| *8s* | *4s* | *2s* | *1s* |
|---|---|---|---|
| *($2^3$)* | *($2^2$)* | *($2^1$)* | *($2^0$)* |
| 1 | 1 | 0 | 1 |

The binary number 1101 is therefore equivalent to the decimal number 13, since $(1 \times 8) + (1 \times 4) + (1 \times 1) = 13$.

**binary search** rapid technique used to find any particular record in a list of records held in sequential order. The computer is programmed to compare the record sought with the record in the middle of the ordered list. This being done, the computer discards the half of the list in which the record does not appear, thereby reducing the number of records left to search by half. This process of selecting the middle record and discarding the unwanted half of the list is repeated until the required record is found.

**biological computer** proposed technology for computing devices based on growing complex organic molecules (biomolecules) as components. Its theoretical basis is that cells, the building blocks of all living things, have chemical systems that can store and exchange electrons and therefore function as electrical components. It is currently the subject of long-term research.

**bistable circuit** or *flip-flop* simple electronic circuit that remains in one of two stable states until it receives a pulse (logic 1 signal) through one of its inputs, upon which it switches, or 'flips', over to the other state. Because it is a two-state device, it can be used to store binary digits and is widely used in the ▷integrated circuits used to build computers.

**bit** (contraction of *binary digit*) single binary digit, either 0 or 1. A bit is the smallest unit of data stored in a computer; all other data must be coded into a pattern of individual bits. A ▷byte represents sufficient computer memory to store a single ▷character of data, and usually contains eight bits. For example, in most computers the capital letter A would be stored in a single byte of memory as the bit pattern 01000001.

The maximum number of bits that a computer can normally process at one time is called a *word*. Microcomputers are often described according to how many bits of information they can handle at once. For instance, the first microprocessor, the Intel 4004 (launched 1971), was a 4-bit device. In the 1970s several different 8-bit computers, many based on the Zilog Z80 or Rockwell 6502 processors, came into common use. During the early 1980s, the IBM personal computer was introduced, using the Intel 8088 processor, which combined a 16-bit processor with an 8-bit ▷data bus. Business micros of the later 1980s began to use 32-bit processors such as the Intel 80386 and Motorola 68030. In the early 1990s 64-bit microprocessors first went into production.

**block** group of ▷records treated as a complete unit for transfer to or from ▷backing storage. For example, many disc drives transfer data in 512-byte blocks.

**boot** or *bootstrap* the process of starting up a computer. Most computers have a small, built-in boot program that starts automatically when the computer is switched on—its only task is to load a slightly larger program, usually from a disc, which in turn loads the main ◊operating system. In microcomputers the operating system is frequently held in the permanent ◊ROM memory and the boot program simply triggers its operation.

Some boot programs can be customized so that, for example, the computer, when switched on, always loads and runs a program from a particular backing store or always adopts a particular mode of screen display.

**bubble memory** memory device based on the creation of small 'bubbles' on a magnetic surface. Bubble memories typically store up to 4 megabits (4 million ◊bits) of information. They are not sensitive to shock and vibration, unlike other memory devices such as disc drives, yet, like magnetic discs, they are non-volatile and do not lose their information when the computer is switched off.

**bubble sort** technique for ◊sorting data. Adjacent items are continually exchanged until the data are in sequence.

**buffer** a part of the ◊memory used to store data temporarily while they are waiting to be used. For example, a program might store data in a printer buffer until the printer is ready to print them.

**bug** an ◊error in a program. It can be an error in the logical structure of a program or a syntax error, such as a spelling mistake. Some bugs cause a program to fail immediately; others remain dormant, causing problems only when a particular combination of events occurs. The process of finding and removing errors from a program is called *debugging*.

**bureau** organization that offers a range of computer services, such as payroll processing or specialized printing. The use of bureaux has declined as computer hardware has become cheaper and more companies have obtained their own computer systems.

**bus** the electrical pathway through which a computer processor com-

## bus

*bus arrangement in a typical microcomputer*

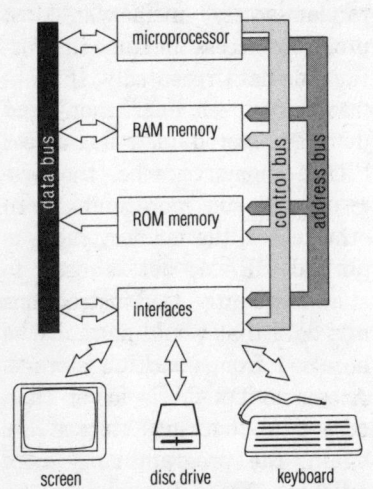

municates with some of its parts and/or peripherals. Physically, a bus is a set of parallel tracks that can carry digital signals; it may take the form of copper tracks laid down on the computer's ◊printed circuit boards (PCBs), or of an external cable or connection.

A computer typically has three internal buses laid down on its main circuit board: a ***data bus***, which carries data between the components of the computer; an ***address bus***, which selects the route to be followed by any particular data item travelling along the data bus; and a ***control bus***, which is used to decide whether data is written to or read from the data bus. An external ***expansion bus*** is used for linking the computer processor to peripheral devices, such as modems and printers.

**byte** sufficient computer memory to store a single ◊character of data. The character is stored in the byte of memory as a pattern of ◊bits (binary digits), using a code such as ◊ASCII. A byte usually contains eight bits—for example, the capital letter F can be stored as the bit pattern 11000110.

A single byte can specify 256 values, such as the decimal numbers from 0 to 255; in the case of a single-byte ◊pixel (picture element), it can specify 256 different colours. Three bytes (24 bits) can specify 16,777,216 values. Computer memory size is measured in ***kilobytes*** (1,024 bytes) or ***megabytes*** (1,024 kilobytes).

**C** high-level general-purpose programming language popular on minicomputers and microcomputers. Developed in the early 1970s from an earlier language called BCPL, C was first used as the language of the operating system ◊Unix, though it has since become widespread beyond Unix. It is useful for writing fast and efficient applications programs, such as ◊operating systems.

**cache memory** a reserved area of the ◊immediate-access memory used to increase the running speed of a computer program.

The cache memory may be constructed from ◊SRAM (static random-access memory), which is faster but more expensive than the normal ◊DRAM (dynamic random-access memory). Most programs access the same instructions or data repeatedly. If these frequently used instructions and data are stored in a fast-access SRAM memory cache, the program will run more quickly. In other cases, the memory cache is normal DRAM, but is used to store frequently used instructions and data that would normally be accessed from ◊backing storage. Access to DRAM is faster than access to backing storage so, again, the program runs more quickly. This type of cache memory is often called a ***disc cache***.

**CAD** (acronym for *c*omputer-*a*ided *d*esign) the use of computers in creating and editing design drawings. CAD also allows such things as automatic testing of designs and multiple or animated three-dimensional views of designs. CAD systems are widely used in architecture, electronics, and engineering, for example in the motor-vehicle industry, where cars designed with the assistance of computers are now commonplace. A related development is

▷CAM (computer-assisted manufacture).

**CAL** (acronym for *c*omputer-*a*ssisted *l*earning) the use of computers in education and training: the computer displays instructional material to a student and asks questions about the information given; the student's answers determine the sequence of the lessons.

**CAM** (acronym for *c*omputer-*a*ided *m*anufacture) the use of computers to control production processes; in particular, the control of machine tools and ▷robots in factories. In some factories, the whole design and production system has been automated by linking ▷CAD (computer-aided design) to CAM.

**CAT scan** or *CT scan* (acronym for *c*omputerized *a*xial *t*omography) in medicine, a sophisticated method of X-ray imaging. Quick and non-invasive, CAT scanning is an aid to diagnosis, helping to pinpoint problem areas without the need for exploratory surgery.

The CAT scanner passes a narrow fan of X-rays through successive slices of the suspect body part. These slices are picked up by crystal detectors in a scintillator and converted electronically into cross-sectional images displayed on a viewing screen. Gradually, using views taken from various angles, a three-dimensional picture of the organ or tissue can be built up and suspect irregularities analysed.

**CD-ROM** (abbreviation for *compact-disc read-only memory*) computer storage device developed from the technology of the audio compact disc. It consists of a plastic-coated metal disc, on which binary digital information is etched in the form of microscopic pits. This can then be read optically by passing a light beam over the disc. CD-ROMs typically hold about 550 ▷megabytes of data, and are used in distributing large amounts of text and graphics, such as encyclopedias, catalogues, and technical manuals.

Standard CD-ROMs cannot have information written onto them by computer, but must be manufactured from a master. Although recordable CDs, called ▷WORMs ('write once, read many times'), have been developed for use as computer discs, they are as yet too expensive for use by private individuals. A compact disc that can be overwritten repeatedly by a computer has also been developed; see ◊optical disc. The compact disc, with its enormous storage capability, may eventually replace the magnetic disc as the most common form of backing store for computers.

**Ceefax** ('see facts') one of Britain's two ◊teletext systems, or 'magazines of the air', developed by the BBC and first broadcast in 1973. See also ◊Oracle.

**central processing unit** (CPU) the main component of a computer, the part that executes individual program instructions and controls the operation of other parts. It is sometimes called the central processor or, when contained on a single integrated circuit, a microprocessor.

The CPU has three main components: the *arithmetic and logic unit* (ALU), where all calculations and logical operations are carried out; a *control unit*, which decodes, synchronizes, and executes program instructions; and the *immediate-access memory*,

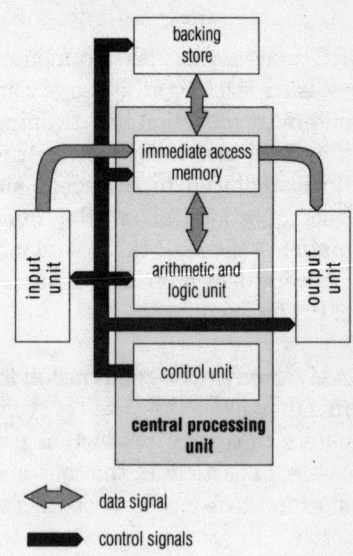

*central processing unit*

which stores the data and programs on which the computer is currently working. All these components contain ◊registers, which are memory locations reserved for specific purposes.

These registers include the ◊accumulator, ◊instruction register, and ◊sequence-control register.

**Centronics interface** standard type of computer ◊interface, used to connect computers to ◊parallel devices.

**character** one of the symbols that can be represented in a computer. Characters include letters, numbers, spaces, punctuation marks, and special symbols.

**character printer** computer ◊printer that prints one character at a time.

**character set** the complete set of symbols that can be used in a program or recognized by a computer. It may include letters, digits, spaces, punctuation marks, and special symbols.

**character type check** a ◊validation check to ensure that an input data item does not contain invalid characters. For example, an input name may be checked to ensure that it contains only letters of the alphabet or an input six-figure date may be checked to ensure it contains only numbers.

**check digit** a digit attached to an important code number as a ◊validation check.

**chip** or *silicon chip* another name for an ◊*integrated circuit*, a complete electronic circuit on a slice of silicon (or other semiconductor) crystal measuring only a few millimetres square.

**CISC** (acronym for *c*omplex *i*nstruction *s*et *c*omputer) a microprocessor (processor on a single chip) that can carry out a large number of ◊machine-code instructions—for example, the Intel 80386. The term was introduced to distinguish them from the more rapid ◊RISC (*r*educed *i*nstruction *s*et *c*omputer) processors, which handle only a smaller set of instructions.

**client–server architecture** a system in which the mechanics of storing data are separated from the programs that use the data. For example, the 'server' might be a central database, typically located on a large computer that is reserved for this purpose. The 'client' would be an ordinary program that requests data from the server as needed. See also ◊SQL.

**clock interrupt** an ◊interrupt signal generated by the computer's internal electronic clock.

**clock rate** the frequency of a computer's internal electronic clock. Every computer contains an electronic clock, which produces a sequence of regular electrical pulses used by the control unit to synchronize the components of the computer and regulate the ◊fetch–execute cycle by which program instructions are processed. A fixed number of time pulses is required in order to execute each particular instruction. The speed at which a computer can process instructions therefore depends on the clock rate: increasing the clock rate will decrease the time required to complete each particular instruction.

Clock rates are measured in **megahertz** (MHz), or millions of pulses a second. Microcomputers commonly have a clock rate of 4–20 MHz.

**CMOS** abbreviation for ◊*complementary metal-oxide semiconductor* family of integrated circuits (chips) widely used in building electronic systems.

**CNC** abbreviation for ◊*computer numerical control*.

**COBOL** (acronym for *co*mmon *b*usiness-*o*riented *l*anguage) high-level programming language, which was designed in the 1950s for commercial data-processing problems; it has become one of the major languages in this field. COBOL features powerful facilities for file handling and business arithmetic. Program instructions written in this language make extensive use of words and look very much like English sentences. This makes COBOL one of the easiest languages to learn and understand.

**COM** acronym for ◊*computer output on microfilm/microfiche*.

**command language** set of commands and the rules governing their use, by which users control a program. For example, an ◊operating system may have commands such as SAVE and DELETE, or a payroll program may have commands for adding and amending staff records.

**compiler** computer program that translates programs written in a ◊high-level language into machine code (the form in which they can be run by the computer). The compiler translates each high-level instruction into several machine-code instructions—in a process called **compilation**—and produces a complete independent

*compiler*

*flowchart showing how a compiler works*

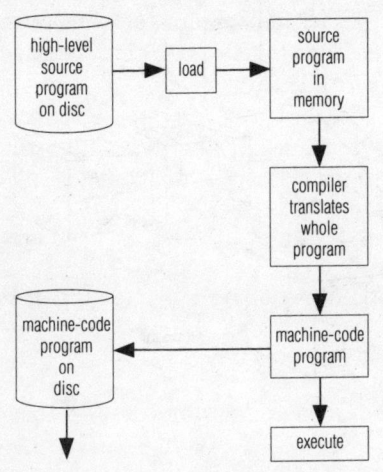

program that can be run by the computer as often as required, without the original source program being present.

Different compilers are needed for different high-level languages and for different computers. In contrast to using an ◊interpreter, using a compiler adds slightly to the time needed to develop a new program because the machine-code program must be recompiled after each change or correction. Once compiled, however, the program will run much faster than an interpreted program.

**complementary metal-oxide semiconductor** (CMOS) a particular way of manufacturing integrated circuits (chips). The main advantage of CMOS chips is their low power requirement and heat dissipation, which enables them to be used in electronic watches and portable microcomputers. However, CMOS circuits are expensive to manufacture and have lower operating speeds than have circuits of the ◊transistor–transistor logic (TTL) family.

**computer** programmable electronic device that can input, store, process, and output data. Almost all modern computers are ◊digital computers, which store and process data using ◊binary number codes. As a result of research and development, the size, speed, and capability of computers is always changing. A computer that, only a few years ago, might have been considered fast and powerful may today be considered obsolete; see ◊computer generation.

Computers can be divided into four main types, corresponding roughly to their size and intended use:

***Microcomputers*** are the most

*computer*
typical mainframe computer system

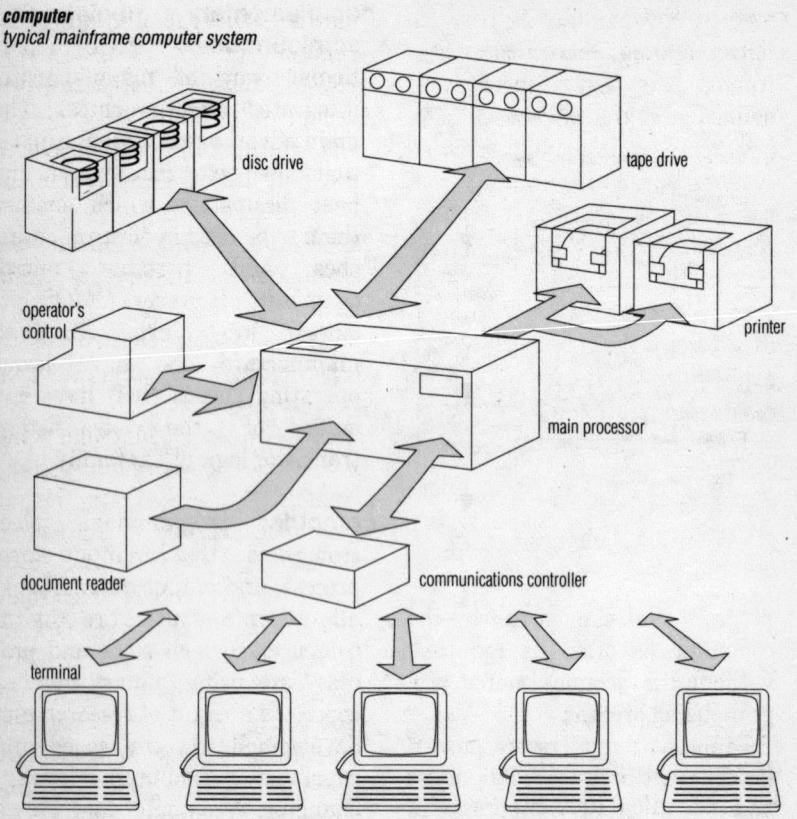

common and the smallest type, used in businesses, at home, and in schools. They are usually single-user machines, but can also be connected together to form local area ◊networks (LANs).

**Mainframes**, which can often service several hundreds of users simultaneously, are found in large organizations, such as government departments.

**Minicomputers** were originally developed as smaller, cheaper, less well-equipped alternatives to mainframe computers. They may support from 10 to 200 or so users at once. The dividing line between minicomputers and small mainframes has never been well defined and the advent of more powerful microcomputer-based systems that rival minicomputers has made the term even less clear.

**Supercomputers** are capable of very high computing speeds. They are used for highly complex scientific tasks, such as analysing the results of nuclear physics experiments and weather forecasting.

*computer history*

*1614* John Napier invented logarithms.

*1615* William Oughtred invented the slide rule.

*1623* Wilhelm Schickard invented the mechanical calculating machine.

*1645* Blaise Pascal produced a calculator.

*1672–74* Gottfried Leibniz built his first calculator, the Stepped Reckoner.

*1801* Joseph-Marie Jacquard developed an automatic loom controlled by punch cards.

*1820* The first mass-produced calculator, the Arithometer, was developed by Charles Thomas de Colmar.

*1822* Charles Babbage completed his first model for the difference engine.

*1830s* Babbage created the first design for the analytical engine.

*1890* Herman Hollerith developed the punched-card reader for the US census.

*1936* Alan Turing published the mathematical theory of computing.

*1938* Konrad Zuse constructed the first binary calculator, using Boolean algebra.

*1939* US mathematician and physicist J V Atanasoff became the first to use electronic means for mechanizing arithmetical operations.

*1943* The Colossus electronic code-breaker was developed at Bletchley Park, England. The Harvard University Mark I or Automatic Sequence Controlled Calculator (partly financed by IBM) became the first program-controlled calculator.

*1946* ENIAC (acronym for *e*lectronic *n*umerator, *i*ntegrator, *a*nalyser, and *c*omputer), the first general-purpose, fully electronic digital computer, was completed at the University of Pennsylvania, USA.

*1948* Manchester University (England) Mark I, the first stored-program computer, was completed. William Shockley of Bell Laboratories invented the transistor.

*1951* Launch of Ferranti Mark I, the first commercially produced computer. Whirlwind, the first real-time computer, was built for the US air-defence system. Grace Murray Hopper of Remington Rand invented the compiler computer program.

*1952* EDVAC (acronym for electronic discrete variable computer) was completed at the Institute for Advanced Study, Princeton, USA (by John Von Neumann and others).

*1953* Magnetic core memory was developed.

*1958* The first integrated circuit was constructed.

*1963* The first minicomputer was built by Digital Equipment (DEC). PDP-8, the first electronic calculator, was built by Bell Punch Company.

*1964* Launch of IBM System/360, the first compatible family of computers. John Kemeny and Thomas Kurtz of Dartmouth College invented BASIC (Beginner's All-purpose Symbolic Instruction Code), a computer language similar to FORTRAN.

*1965* The first supercomputer, the Control Data CD6600, was developed.

*1971* The first microprocessor, the Intel 4004, was announced.

*1974* CLIP-4, the first computer with a parallel architecture, was developed by IBM.

*1975* The first microcomputer, Altair 8800, was launched.

*1981* The Xerox Star system, the first graphical user-interface system, was developed.

*1985* The Inmos T414 transputer, the first 'off-the-shelf' microprocessor for building parallel computers, was announced.

*1988* The first optical microchip was developed.

*1989* Wafer-scale silicon memory chips, able to store 200 million characters, were launched.

*1990* Microsoft released Windows 3, a windowing environment for PCs.

*1991* IBM developed the world's fastest high-capacity memory computer chip, SRAM (static random-access memory), able to send or receive 8 billion bits of information per second.

**computer-aided design** use of computers to create and modify design drawings; see ◊CAD.

**computer-aided manufacture** use of computers to regulate production processes in industry; see ◊CAM.

**computer-assisted learning** use of computers in education and training; see ◊CAL.

**computer engineer** job classification for ◊computer personnel. A computer engineer repairs and maintains computer hardware.

**computer game** or *video game* any computer-controlled game in which the computer (usually) opposes the human player. Computer games typically employ fast, animated graphics on a ◊visual display unit (VDU), and synthesized sound.

Commercial computer games became possible with the advent of the ◊microprocessor in the mid-1970s and rapidly became popular in the form of amusement-arcade games, using dedicated chips. Currently available games range from chess to fighter-plane simulations.

**computer generation** any of the five broad groups into which computers may be classified:

*first generation* the earliest computers, developed in the 1940s and 1950s, made from valves and wire circuits;

*second generation* from the early 1960s, based on transistors and printed circuits;

*third generation* from the late 1960s, using integrated circuits and often sold as families of computers, such as the IBM 360 series;

*fourth generation* using ◊microprocessors and large-scale integration, still in use in the 1990s; and

*fifth generation* based on parallel processors and very large-scale integration, not yet commercially available.

**computer graphics** use of computers to display and manipulate information in pictorial form. The output may be as simple as a pie chart, or as complex as an animated sequence in a science-fiction film or a seemingly three-dimensional engineering blueprint. Input may be achieved by drawing with a mouse or stylus on a graphics tablet, or by drawing directly on the screen with a light pen. The drawing is stored in the computer as ◊raster graphics

# computer numerical control

*computer graphics*

*vector graphics display before and after transformation*

*raster graphics display before and after transformation*

or ◊vector graphics. Computer graphics are increasingly used in computer-aided design (◊CAD), and to generate models and simulations in engineering, meteorology, medicine and surgery, and other fields of science.

**computer numerical control** control of machine tools, most often milling machines, by a computer. The pattern of work for the machine to follow, which often involves performing repeated sequences of actions, is described using a special-purpose programming language.

**computer operator** job classification for ◊computer personnel. Computer operators work directly with the computer, running the programs, changing discs and tapes, loading paper into printers, and ensuring all ◊data security procedures are followed.

**computer output on microfilm/ microfiche** (COM) technique for producing computer output in very compact, photographically reduced form (◊microform).

**computer personnel** people who work with or are associated with computers. In a large computer department the staff may work under the direction of a ***data processing manager***, who supervises and coordinates the work performed. Computer personnel can be broadly divided into two categories: those who run and maintain existing ◊applications programs that perform a task for the benefit of the user, and those who develop new applications.

*computer personnel*

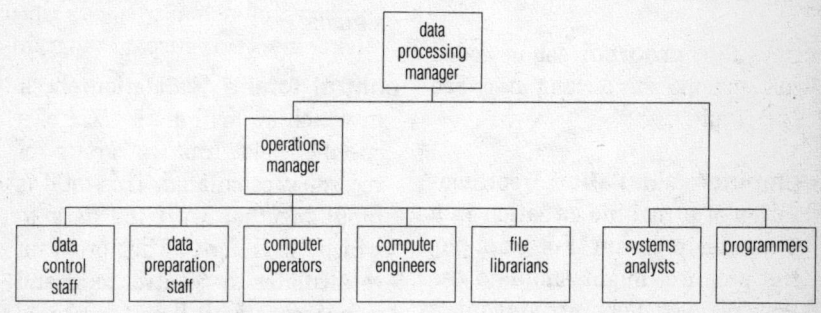

Personnel who run existing applications programs:

***data control staff*** receive information from computer users (for instance, from the company's wages clerks), ensure that it is processed as required, and return it to them in processed form;

***data preparation staff***, or ***keyboard operators***, prepare the information received by the data control staff so that it is ready for processing by computer. Once the information has been typed at the keyboard of a VDU (or at a ◊key-to-disc or key-to-tape station), it is placed directly onto a medium such as disc or tape;

***computer operators*** work directly with computers, running the programs, changing discs and tapes, loading paper into printers, and ensuring that all ◊data security procedures are followed;

***computer engineers*** repair and maintain computer hardware;

***file librarians***, or ***media librarians***, store and issue the data files used by the department; an ***operations manager*** coordinates all the day-to-day activities of these staff.

Personnel who develop new applications:

***systems analysts*** carry out the analysis of an existing system (see ◊systems analysis), whether already computerized or not, and prepare proposals for a new computerized system;

**computer programmers** write the software needed for new systems.

**computer program** set of coded instructions for a computer; see ◊program.

**computer simulation** representation of a real-life situation in a computer program. For example, the program might simulate the flow of customers arriving at a bank. The user can alter variables, such as the number of cashiers on duty, and see the effect.

More complex simulations can model the behaviour of chemical reactions or even nuclear explosions.

Computers also control the actions of machines—for example, a ◊flight simulator models the behaviour of real aircraft and allows training to take place in safety.

Computer simulations are extremely useful when it is too dangerous, time consuming, or simply impossible to carry out a real experiment or test.

**computer terminal** the device whereby the operator communicates with the computer; see ◊terminal.

**control bus** electrical pathway, or ◊bus, used to communicate control signals.

**control total** a ◊validation check in which an arithmetic total of a specific field from a group of records is calculated. This total is input together with the data to which it refers. The program recalculates the control total and compares it with the one entered to ensure that no entry errors have been made.

**control unit** the component of the ◊central processing unit that decodes, synchronizes, and executes program instructions.

**corruption of data** introduction or presence of errors in data. Most computers use a range of ◊verification and ◊validation routines to prevent corrupt data from entering the computer system or detect corrupt data that are already present.

**CP/M** (abbreviation for *control program/monitor* or *control program for microcomputers*) one of the earliest ◊operating systems for microcomputers. It was produced by Digital Research Corporation, and became a standard for microcomputers based on the Intel 8080 and Zilog Z80 8-bit microprocessors. In the 1980s it was superseded by ◊MS-DOS, written for 16-bit microprocessors.

**CPU** abbreviation for ◊central processing unit.

**critical path analysis** procedure used in the management of complex projects to minimize the amount of time taken. The analysis shows which subprojects can run in parallel with each other, and which have to be completed before other subprojects can follow on. By identifying the time required for each separate subproject and the relationship between the subprojects, it is possible to produce a planning schedule showing when each subproject should be started and finished in order to complete the whole project most efficiently. Complex projects may involve hundreds of subprojects and computer ◊applications packages for critical path analysis are widely used to help reduce the time and effort involved in their analysis.

**cursor** on a computer screen, the symbol that indicates the current entry position (position where the next character will appear). It usually consists of a solid rectangle or underline character, flashing on and off.

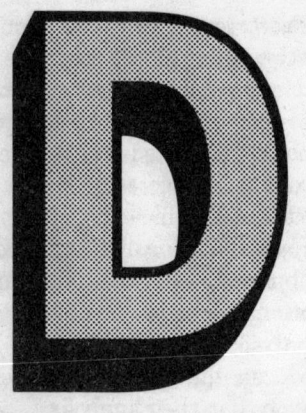

**DAC** abbreviation for ◊*digital-to-analogue converter*.

**daisywheel printer** computer printer in which the printing head consists of a small plastic or metal disc made up of many spokes (like the petals of a daisy). At the end of each spoke is a character in relief.

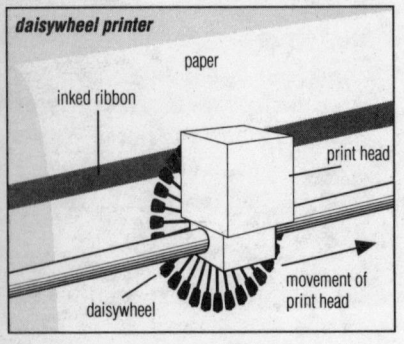

*daisywheel printer*

The daisywheel is rotated until the spoke bearing the required character is facing an inked ribbon, then a hammer strikes the spoke against the ribbon, leaving the impression of the character on the paper beneath.

The daisywheel can be changed to provide different typefaces; however, daisywheel printers cannot print graphics nor can they easily print more than one typeface in the same document. For these reasons, they are rapidly becoming obsolete.

**data** facts, figures, and symbols, especially as stored in computers. The term is often used to mean raw, unprocessed facts, as distinct from information, to which a meaning or interpretation has been applied.

**database** structured collection of data. The database makes data available to the various programs that need them, without the need for those programs to be aware of how the data are stored.

There are three main types (or 'models') of database: hierarchical, network, and ◊relational, of which relational is the most widely used.

A *free-text database* is one that holds the unstructured text of articles or books in a form that permits rapid searching. A collection of databases is known as a *databank*.

A database-management system (DBMS) program ensures that the integrity of the data is maintained by controlling the degree of access of the ◊applications programs that use the data. Databases are normally used by large organizations with mainframes or minicomputers.

A telephone directory stored as a database might allow all the people whose names start with the letter B to be selected by one program, and all those living in Chicago by another.

**data bus** the electrical pathway, or ◊bus, used to carry data between the components of the computer.

**data capture** collecting information for computer processing and analysis. Data may be captured either automatically—for example, by a ◊sensor that continuously monitors physical conditions such as temperature, or manually—for example, by reading electricity meters.

**data communications** sending and receiving data via any communications medium, such as a telephone line. The term usually implies that the data are digital (such as computer data) rather than analogue (such as voice messages). However, in the ISDN (◊integrated services digital network) system, all data are transmitted digitally.

**data compression** techniques for reducing the amount of storage needed for a given amount of data. They include word tokenization (in which frequently used words are stored as shorter codes), variable bit lengths (in which common characters are represented by fewer ◊bits than less common ones), and run-length encoding (in which a repeated value is stored once along with a count).

**data control staff** job classification for ◊computer personnel. Data control staff receive information from computer users, ensure that it is processed as required, and return it to them in processed form.

**data flow chart** diagram illustrating the possible routes that data can take through a system or program; see ◊flow chart.

**data input** entering data into a computer system.

**data logging** the process, usually automatic, of capturing and recording a sequence of values for later processing and analysis by computer. For example, the level in a water-storage tank might be automatically logged every hour over a seven-day period, so that a computer could produce an analysis of water use.

**data preparation** preparing data for computer input by transferring it to a machine-readable medium. This usually involves typing the data at a keyboard (or at a ◊key-to-disc or key-to-tape station) so that it can be transferred directly to tapes or discs. Various methods of direct data capture, such as ◊bar codes, ◊optical mark recognition (OMR), and ◊optical character recognition (OCR), have been developed to reduce or eliminate lengthy data preparation before input.

**data preparation staff** job classification for ◊computer personnel. Data preparation staff prepare information so that it is ready for processing by computer. This often entails typing the data at a keyboard so that it can be transferred to a computer medium (see ◊media) such as a disc or tape.

**data processing** (DP) use of computers for performing clerical tasks such as stock control, payroll, and dealing with orders. DP systems are typically ◊batch processing systems, running on mainframe computers. DP is sometimes called EDP (electronic data processing).

A large organization usually has a special department to support its DP activities, which might include the writing and maintenance of software (programs), control and operation of the computers, and an analysis of the organization's information requirements. See also ◊computer personnel.

**data processing manager** job classification for ◊computer personnel. A data processing manager supervises and coordinates the work of the computer department.

**data protection** safeguarding of information about individuals stored on computers, to protect privacy. The Council of Europe adopted, in 1981, a Data Protection Convention, which led in the UK to the Data Protection Act 1984. This requires computer databases containing personal information to be registered, and users to process accurate information only and to retain the information only for a necessary period and for specified purposes. Subject to certain exemptions, individuals have a right of access to their personal data and to have any errors corrected.

**data security** precautions taken to prevent the loss or misuse of data, whether accidental or deliberate. These include measures that ensure that only authorized personnel can gain entry to a computer system or file, and regular procedures for storing data, which enable files to be retrieved or recreated in the event of loss, theft, or damage. A number of ◊verification and ◊validation techniques may also be employed to prevent data from being lost or corrupted by misprocessing.

***Encryption*** involves the translation of data into a form that is meaningless to unauthorized users who do not have the necessary decoding software.

***Passwords*** can be chosen by, or issued to, individual users. These secret words (or combinations of alphanumeric characters) may have to be entered each time a user logs on to a computer system or attempts to access a particular protected file.

***Physical access*** to the computer facilities can be restricted through the locking of entry doors and storage cabinets.

***Master files*** (files that are updated periodically) can be protected by storing successive versions, or ***generations***, of these files and of the transaction files used to update them. The most recent version of the master file may then be recreated, if necessary, from a previous generation. It is common practice to store the three most recent versions of a master file (often called the grandfather, father, and son generations).

***Direct-access files*** are protected by making regular ***dumps***, or copies. Because the individual records in direct-access files are constantly being accessed and

## data terminator

***data security***
*write protection*

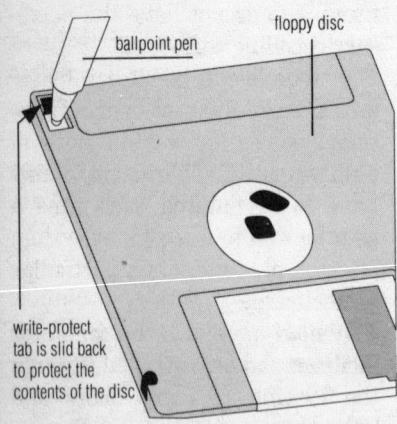

ballpoint pen
floppy disc
write-protect tab is slid back to protect the contents of the disc

updated, specific generations of these files cannot be said to exist. The files are therefore dumped at fixed time intervals onto a secure form of backing store. A record, or log, is also kept of all the changes that are made to a file between security dumps.

*Fireproof safes* are used to store file generations or sets of security dumps, so that the system can be restarted on a new computer in the event of a fire in the computer department.

*Write-protect* mechanisms on discs or tapes allow data to be read but not deleted, altered, or overwritten. For example, the protective case of a 3½-inch floppy disc has a write-protect tab that can be slid back with the tip of a pencil or pen to protect the disc's contents.

**data terminator** or *rogue value* a special value used to mark the end of a list of input data items. The computer must be able to detect that the data terminator is different from the input data in some way—for instance, a negative number might be used to signal the end of a list of positive numbers, or 'XXX' might be used to terminate the entry of a list of names.

**dBASE** family of microcomputer programs used for manipulating large quantities of data. The term also refers to a related ▷fourth-generation language, the first version of which, dBASE II, appeared in 1981. dBASE II has since become a recognized standard for database applications.

**debugging** finding and removing errors, or ▷bugs, from a computer program or system.

**decimal number system** or *denary number system* the most commonly used number system, to the base ten. Decimal numbers do not necessarily contain a decimal point; 563, 5.63, and −563 are all decimal numbers. Other systems are mainly used in computing and include the ◊binary number system, ◊octal number system, and ◊hexadecimal number system.

Decimal numbers may be thought of as written under column headings based on the number ten. For example, the number 2,567 stands for:

| 1,000s | 100s | 10s | 1s |
|---|---|---|---|
| $(10^3)$ | $(10^2)$ | $(10^1)$ | $(10^0)$ |
| 2 | 5 | 6 | 7 |

Large decimal numbers may also be expressed in ◊floating-point notation.

**decision table** a method of describing a procedure for a program to follow, based on comparing possible decisions and their consequences. It is often used as an aid in systems design.

The top part of the table contains the conditions for making decisions (for example, if a number is negative rather than positive and is less than 1), and the bottom part describes the outcomes when those conditions are met. The program either ends or repeats the operation.

**decoder** an electronic circuit used to select one of several possible data pathways. Decoders are, for example, used to direct data to individual memory locations within a computer's immediate access memory.

**dedicated computer** computer built into another device for the purpose of controlling or supplying information to it. Its use has increased dramatically since the advent of the ◊microprocessor: washing machines, digital watches, cars, and video recorders all now have their own processors.

A dedicated system is a type of general-purpose computer system confined to performing only one function for reasons of efficiency or convenience. A word processor is an example.

**desktop publishing** (DTP) use of microcomputers for small-scale typesetting and page make-up. DTP systems are capable of producing camera-ready pages (pages ready for photographing and printing), made up of text and graphics, with text set in different typefaces and sizes. The page can be previewed on the screen before final printing on a laser printer.

**digit** any of the numbers from 0 to 9. Different numbering systems have different ranges of digits. For example, the ◊hexadecimal number system has digits 0 to 9 and A to F, whereas the binary number system has two digits (or ◊bits), 0 and 1.

**digital** (of a quantity or device) changing in a series of distinct steps; by contrast, an ◊analogue quantity or device varies continuously. For example, a digital clock measures time with a numerical display that changes in a series of discrete steps, whereas an analogue clock measures time by means of a continuous movement of hands around a dial.

Computers are digital devices because their electronic circuits can distinguish between just two values, 0 and 1 (representing two states: on and off, or high-voltage and low-voltage pulses). All the data that a computer stores, processes, and transmits must therefore be encoded digitally, as a series of 0s and 1s, in ◊binary number code.

**digital computer** computing device that operates on a two-state system, using symbols that are internally coded as binary numbers (numbers made up of combinations of the digits 0 and 1); see ◊computer.

**digital data transmission** a way of sending data by converting all signals (whether pictures, sounds, or words) into numeric (normally binary) codes before transmission, then reconverting them on receipt. This virtually eliminates any distortion or degradation of the signal during transmission, storage, or processing.

**digital-to-analogue converter** electronic circuit that converts a digital signal into an ◊analogue (continuously varying) signal. Such a circuit is used to convert the digital output from a computer into the analogue voltage required to produce sound from a conventional loudspeaker.

**digitizer** a device that converts an analogue video signal into a digital format so that video images can be input, stored, displayed, and manipulated by a computer.

*disc*
*cut-away view of a removable pack of hard discs in a drive unit*

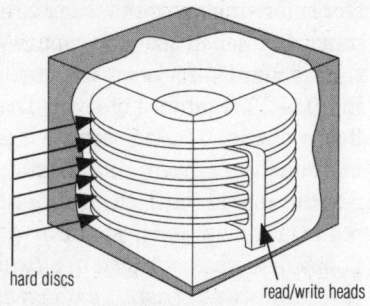

hard discs    read/write heads

The term is sometimes used to refer to a ◊graphics tablet.

**direct access** or ***random access*** type of ◊file access. A direct-access file contains records that can be accessed directly by the computer because each record has its own address on the storage disc.

**direct data entry** data preparation using a ◊key-to-disc or key-to-tape system.

**directory** a list of file names, together with information that enables a computer to retrieve those files from ◊backing storage. The computer operating system will usually store and update a directory on the backing storage to which it refers. So, for example, on each ◊disc used by a computer a directory file will be created listing the disc's contents.

**disc** a common medium for storing large volumes of data (an alternative is ◊magnetic tape). A ***magnetic disc*** is rotated at high speed in a disc-drive unit as a read/write (playback or record) head passes over its surfaces to record or read the magnetic variations that encode the data. Recently, ***optical discs***, such as ◊CD-ROM (compact-disc read-only memory) and ◊WORM (write once, read many times), have been used to store computer data. Data are recorded on the disc surface as etched microscopic pits and are read by a laser-scanning device. Optical discs have an enormous capacity—about 550 megabytes (million ◊bytes) on a compact disc, and thousands of megabytes on a full-size optical disc.

Magnetic discs come in several forms:
***Fixed hard discs*** are built into the disc-drive unit, occasionally stacked on top of one another. A fixed disc cannot be removed: once it is full, data must be deleted in order to free space or a complete new disc drive must be added to

the computer system in order to increase storage capacity. Large fixed discs, used with mainframe and minicomputers, provide up to 3,000 megabytes. Small fixed discs for use with microcomputers were introduced in the 1980s and typically hold 40–400 megabytes.

***Removable hard discs*** are common in minicomputer systems. The discs are contained, individually or as stacks (disc packs), in a protective plastic case, and can be taken out of the drive unit and kept for later use. By swapping such discs around, a single hard-disc drive can be made to provide a potentially infinite storage capacity. However, access speeds and capacities tend to be lower that those associated with large fixed hard discs.

A ***floppy disc*** (or diskette) is the most common form of backing store for microcomputers. It is much smaller in size and capacity than a hard disc, normally holding 0.5–2 megabytes of data. The floppy disc is so called because it is manufactured from thin flexible plastic coated with a magnetic material. The earliest form of floppy disc was packaged in a card case and was easily damaged; more recent versions are contained in smaller, rigid plastic cases and are much more robust. All floppy discs can be removed from the drive unit.

**disc drive** mechanical device that reads data from and writes data to a magnetic ▷disc.

**disc formatting** preparing a blank magnetic disc so that data can be stored on it. Data are recorded on a disc's surface on circular tracks, each of which is divided into a number of sectors. In formatting a disc, the computer's operating system adds control information such as track and sector numbers, which enables the data stored to be accessed correctly by the disc-drive unit.

Some hard discs, called ***hard-***

*disc drive*

floppy disc being inserted into disc drive

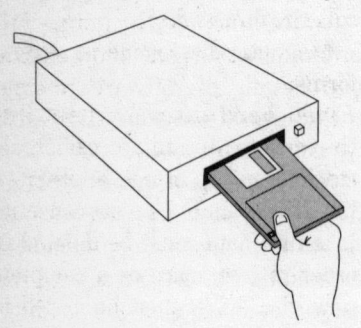

*sectored discs*, are sold already formatted. However, because different makes of computer employ different disc formats, most new discs are sold unformatted, or *soft-sectored*, and computers are provided with the necessary ◊utility program to format these discs correctly before they are used.

**document** data associated with a particular application. For example, a *text document* might be produced by a word processor, and a *graphics document* might be produced by a CAD (computer-aided design) package. An *OMR* (optical mark recognition) or *OCR* (optical character recognition) document is a paper document containing data that can be directly input to the computer using a ◊document reader.

**documentation** the written information associated with a computer program or ◊applications package. Documentation is usually divided into two categories: program documentation and user documentation.

*Program documentation* is the complete technical description of a program, drawn up as the software is written and intended to support any later maintenance or development of that program. It typically includes details of when, where, and by whom the software was written; a general description of the purpose of the software, including recommended input, output, and storage methods; a detailed description of the way the software functions, including full program listings and ◊flow charts; and details of software testing, including sets of ◊test data with expected results.

*User documentation* explains how to operate the software. It typically includes a non-technical explanation of the purpose of the software; instructions for loading,

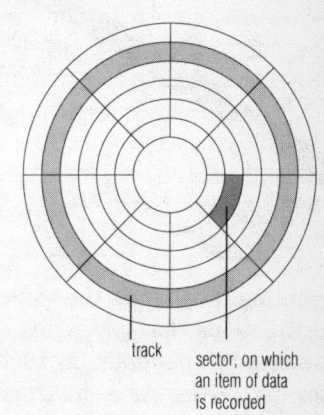

*disc formatting*

surface of a magnetic disc

track — sector, on which an item of data is recorded

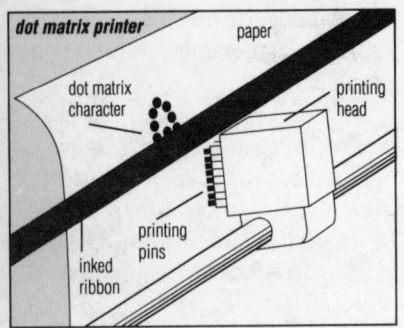
*dot matrix printer*

running, and using the software; instructions for preparing any necessary input data; instructions for requesting and interpreting output data; and explanations of any error messages that the program may produce.

**document reader** an input device that reads marks or characters, usually on preprepared forms and documents. Such devices are used to capture data by ◊optical mark recognition (OMR), ◊optical character recognition (OCR), and ◊mark sensing.

**DOS** (acronym for *d*isc *o*perating *s*ystem) ◊operating system specifically designed for use with disc storage; also used as an alternative name for a particular operating system, ◊MS-DOS.

**dot matrix printer** computer printer that produces each character individually by printing a pattern, or matrix, of very small dots. The printing head consists of a vertical line or block of either 9 or 24 printing pins. As the printing head is moved from side to side across the paper, the pins are pushed forwards selectively to strike an inked ribbon and build up the dot pattern for each character on the paper beneath.

A dot matrix printer is more flexible than a ◊daisywheel printer because it can print graphics and text in many different typefaces. It is cheaper to buy and maintain than a ◊laser printer or ◊ink-jet printer, and, because its pins physically strike the paper, is capable of producing carbon copies. However, it is noisy in operation and cannot produce the high-quality printing associated with these non-impact printers.

**DRAM** (acronym for *d*ynamic *r*andom-*a*ccess *m*emory) memory device in the form of a silicon chip commonly used to provide the ◊immediate-access memory of microcomputers. DRAM loses its contents unless they are read and rewritten every 2 milliseconds or so. This process is known as *refreshing* the memory. DRAM is slower but cheaper than ◊SRAM, an alternative form of silicon-chip memory.

**driver** a program that controls a peripheral device. Every device connected to the computer needs a driver program. The driver ensures that communication between the computer and the device is successful.

For example, it is often possible to connect many different types of printer, each with its own special operating codes, to the same type of computer. This is because driver programs are supplied to translate the computer's standard printing commands into the special commands required for each printer.

**dry running** checking by hand (for example, with paper and pencil) the progress of ◊test data through a computer program, before that program is run on a computer.

**dump** the process of rapidly transferring data to external memory or to a printer. It is usually done to help with debugging (see ◊bug) or as part of an error-recovery procedure designed to provide ◊data security.

A ◊screen dump makes a printed copy of the current screen display.

**EBCDIC** (abbreviation for ***extended binary-coded decimal interchange code***) a code used for storing and communicating alphabetic and numeric characters. It is an 8-bit code, capable of holding 256 different characters, although only 85 of these are defined in the standard version. It is still used in many mainframe computers, but almost all mini- and microcomputers now use ◊ASCII code.

**edge connector** an electrical connection formed by taking some of the metallic tracks on a ◊printed circuit board to the edge of the board and using them to plug directly into a matching socket.

Edge connectors are often used to connect the computer's main circuit board, or motherboard, to the expansion boards that provide the computer with extra memory or other facilities.

Because the tracks making the connection would be very difficult to repair if they were to become worn or damaged, edge connectors should not be used to join components that are regularly connected and disconnected.

**EEPROM** (acronym for *e*lectrically *e*rasable *p*rogrammable *r*ead-*o*nly *m*emory) computer memory that can record data and retain them indefinitely. The data can be erased with an electrical charge and new data recorded.

Some EEPROM must be removed from the computer and erased and reprogrammed using a special device. Other EEPROM, called ***flash memory***, can be erased and reprogrammed without removal from the computer.

**EFTPOS** (acronym for *e*lectronic *f*unds *t*ransfer at *p*oint *o*f *s*ale) transfer of funds from one bank account to another by electronic means. For example, a customer inserts a plastic card into a point-

*electronic mail*

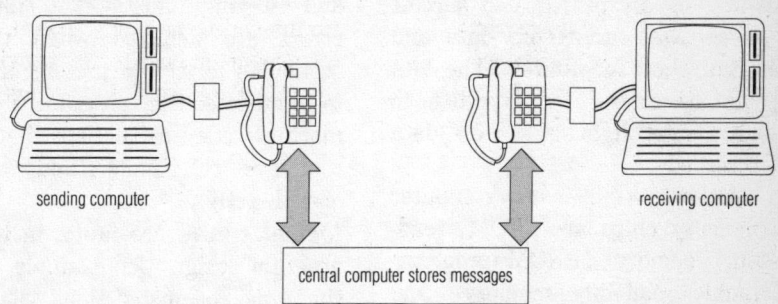

sending computer    central computer stores messages    receiving computer

of-sale computer terminal in a supermarket, and telephone lines are used to make an automatic debit from the customer's bank account to settle the bill.

**electronic mail** or *E-mail* system that enables the users of a computer network to send messages to other users. The messages are usually placed in a reserved area of backing store on a central computer until they are retrieved by the receiving user. Passwords are frequently used to prevent unauthorized access to stored messages (see ◊data security).

**emulator** an item of ◊software or ◊firmware that allows one device to imitate the functioning of another. Emulator software is commonly used to allow one make of computer to run programs written for a different make of computer. This allows a user to select from a wider range of ◊applications programs, and perhaps to save money by running programs designed for an expensive computer on a cheaper model.

Many printers contain emulator firmware that enables them to imitate Hewlett Packard and Epson printers, because so much software is written to work with these widely used machines.

**encryption** providing ◊data security by encoding data so that they are meaningless to unauthorized users who do not have the necessary decoding software.

**EPROM** (acronym for *e*rasable *p*rogrammable *r*ead-*o*nly *m*emory) computer memory device in the form of an ◊integrated circuit (chip) that can record data and retain them indefinitely. The data can be erased by exposure to ultraviolet light, and new data recorded.

Other kinds of computer memory chips are ◊ROM (read-only memory), ◊PROM (programmable read-only memory), and ◊RAM (random-access memory).

**error** a fault or mistake, either in the software or on the part of the user, that causes a program to stop running (crash) or produce unexpected results.

Program errors, or bugs, are largely eliminated in the course of the programmer's initial testing procedure, but some will remain in most programs. All computer operating systems are designed to produce an ***error message*** (on the display screen, or in an error file or printout) whenever an error is detected, reporting that an error has taken place and, wherever possible, diagnosing its cause.

Errors can be categorized into several types:

***syntax errors*** are caused by the incorrect use of the programming language, and include spelling and keying mistakes. These errors are detected when the ◊compiler or ◊interpreter fails to translate the program into machine code (instructions that a computer can understand and obey directly);

***logical errors*** are faults in the program design—for example, in the order of instructions. They may cause a program to respond incorrectly to the user's requests or to crash completely;

***execution errors***, or ***run-time errors***, are caused by combinations of data that the programmer did not anticipate. A typical execution error is caused by attempting to divide a number by zero. This is impossible, and so the program stops running at this point. Execution errors occur only when a program is running, and cannot be detected by a compiler or interpreter.

Computers are designed to deal with a set range of numbers to a given range of accuracy. Many errors are caused by these limitations:

***overflow error*** occurs when a number is too large for the computer to deal with; an ***underflow***

*error* occurs when a number is too small;

***rounding*** and ***truncation errors*** are caused by the need to round off decimal numbers, or to cut them off (truncate them) after the maximum number of decimal places allowed by the computer's level of accuracy.

**error message** message produced by a computer to inform the user that an error has occurred.

**execution error** or ***run-time error*** ◊error caused by combinations of data that the programmer did not anticipate.

**expansion board** or ***expansion card*** printed circuit board that can be inserted into a computer in order to enhance its capabilities (for example, to increase its memory) or to add facilities (such as graphics).

**expert system** computer program for giving advice (such as diagnosing an illness or interpreting the law) that incorporates knowledge derived from human expertise. It is a kind of ◊knowledge-based system containing rules that can be applied to find the solution to a problem. It is a form of ◊artificial intelligence.

**export file** a file stored by the computer in a standard format so that it can be accessed by other programs, possibly running on different makes of computer.

For example, a word-processing program running on an Apple ◊Macintosh computer may have a facility to save a file on a floppy disc in a format that can be read by a word-processing program running on an IBM computer. When the file is being read by the second program, it is often referred to as an ***import file***.

**fax** (common name for *facsimile transmission* or *telefax*) the transmission of images over a telecommunications link, usually the telephone network. When placed on a fax machine, the original image is scanned by a transmitting device and converted into coded signals, which travel via the telephone lines to the receiving fax machine, where an image is created that is a copy of the original. Photographs as well as printed text and drawings can be sent by fax.

**feasibility study** an initial study undertaken by a systems analyst investigating ways of implementing a new computer system. The likely costs and benefits of the system are estimated, and used to form the basis for deciding whether or not to proceed with the implementation of the system.

**feedback** general principle whereby the results produced in an ongoing reaction become factors in modifying or changing the reaction; it is the principle used in self-regulating control systems, ranging from simple thermostats to automatic computer-controlled machine tools. In such systems, information about what *is* happening in a system (such as level of temperature, engine speed, or size of workpiece) is fed back to a controlling device, which compares it with what *should* be happening. If the two are different, the device takes suitable action (such as switching on a heater or resetting the tools). A fully computerized control system, in which there is no operator intervention, is called a *closed-loop feedback* system. A system that also responds to control signals from an operator is called an *open-loop feedback* system.

**fetch–execute cycle** or *processing cycle* the two-phase cycle used by the computer's central processing unit to process the instructions in a program. During the ***fetch phase***, the next program instruction is transferred from the computer's immediate-access memory to the instruction register (memory location used to hold the instruction while it is being executed). During the ***execute phase***, the instruction is decoded and obeyed. The process is repeated in a continuous loop.

**fibre optics** branch of physics dealing with the transmission of light and images through glass or plastic fibres known as ◊optical fibres.

**field** a specific item of data. A field is usually part of a ***record*** which in turn is part of a ◊file.

**field-length check** ◊validation check in which the characters in an input field are counted to ensure that the correct number of characters have been entered. For example, a six-figure date field may be checked to ensure that it does contain exactly six digits.

**fifth-generation computer** anticipated new type of computer based on emerging microelectronic technologies with high computing speeds. The development of very large-scale integration (◊VLSI) technology, which can put many more circuits on to an ◊integrated circuit (chip) than is currently possible, and developments in computer hardware and software design may produce computers far more powerful that those in current use.

It is predicted that a fifth-generation computer will be able to communicate in natural spoken language with its user; store vast knowledge databases; search rapidly through these databases, making intelligent inferences and drawing logical conclusions; and process images and 'see' objects in the way that humans do. See also ◊computer generation.

**file** a collection of data or a program stored in a computer's external memory (for example, on disc). It might include anything from information regarding a company's employees to a program for an adventure game.

Files usually consist of a set of ***records***, each having a number of ***fields*** for specific items of data. For example, the file for a class of

*file*
file structure

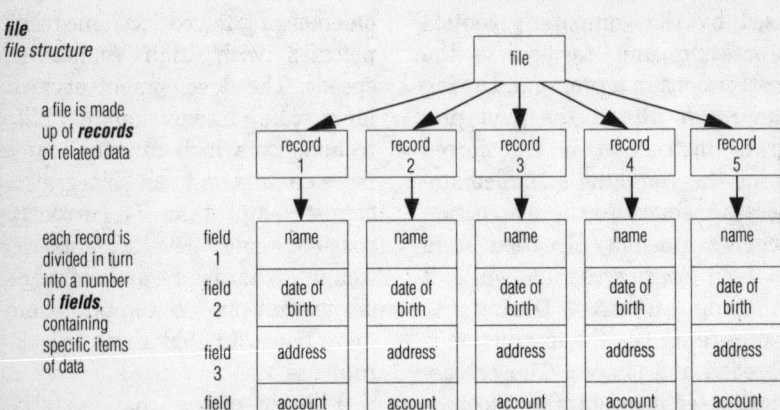

a file is made up of **records** of related data

each record is divided in turn into a number of **fields**, containing specific items of data

schoolchildren might have a record for each child, with five fields of data in each record, storing: (1) family name; (2) first name; (3) house name or number; (4) street name; (5) town. To find out, for example, which children live in the same street, one would look in field 4.

**file access** the way in which the records in a file are stored, retrieved, or updated by computer. There are four main types of file organization, each of which allows a different form of access to the records.

The records in a *serial file* are not stored in any particular order, so a specific record can be accessed only by reading through all the previous records.

Records in a *sequential file* are sorted by reference to a key field (see ◊sorting) and the computer can use a searching technique, such as a ◊binary search, to access a specific record.

An *indexed sequential file* possesses an index, which records the position of each block of records and is created and updated with that file. By consulting the index, the computer can obtain the address of the block containing the required record, and search just that block rather than the whole file.

A *direct-access* or *random-access file* contains records that can be accessed directly by the computer.

**file generation** a specific version of a file. When ▷file updating takes place, a new generation of the file is created, containing accurate, up-to-date information. The old generation of the file will often be stored to provide ▷data security in the event that the new generation is lost or damaged.

**file librarian** or *media librarian* job classification for ▷computer personnel. A file librarian stores and issues the data files used by the computer department.

**file merging** combining two or more sequentially ordered files into a single sequentially ordered file.

**file searching** ▷searching a computer memory for a file.

**file sorting** arranging files in sequence; see ▷sorting.

**file transfer** the transmission of a file (data stored on disc, for example) from one machine to another. Both machines must be physically linked (for example, by

*file updating*
flowchart of the updating of a master file

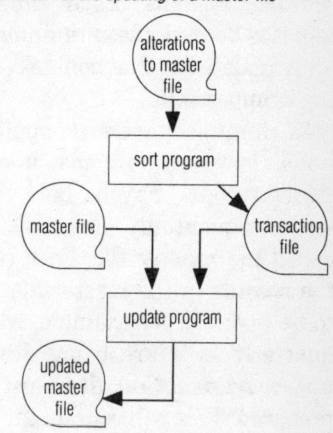

a telephone line via a ▷modem or ▷acoustic coupler) and both must be running appropriate communications software.

**file updating** reviewing and altering the records in a file to ensure that the information they contain is accurate and up-to-date. Three basic processes are involved: adding new records, deleting existing records, and amending existing records.

The updating of a ***direct-access file*** is a continuous process because records can be accessed individually and changed at any time. This type of updating is typical of large interactive database systems, such as airline ticket-booking systems. Each time a ticket is booked, files are immediately updated so that double booking is impossible.

In large commercial applications, however, millions of customer records may be held in a large sequentially ordered file, called the *master file*. Each time the records in the master file are to be updated (for example, when quarterly bills are being drawn up), a *transaction file* must be prepared. This will contain all the additions, deletions, and amendments required to update the master file. The transaction file is sorted into the same order as the master file, and then the computer reads both files and produces a new updated *generation* of the master file, which will be stored until the next file updating takes place.

**firmware** computer program held permanently in a computer's ◊ROM (read-only memory) chips, as opposed to a program that is read in from external memory as it is needed.

**fixed-point notation** system in which numbers are represented using a set of digits with the decimal point always in its correct position. For very large and very small numbers this requires a lot of digits. The size of the numbers that can be handled in this way is limited by the capacity of the computer, and so the slower ◊floating-point notation is often preferred.

**flag** an indicator that can be set or unset in order to signal whether a particular condition is true—for example, whether the end of a file has been reached, or whether an overflow error has occurred. The indicator usually takes the form of a single binary digit, or bit (either 0 or 1).

**flash memory** type of ◊EEPROM memory that can be erased and reprogrammed without removal from the computer.

**flight simulator** a computer-controlled pilot-training device, consisting of an artificial cockpit mounted on hydraulic legs, that simulates the experience of flying a real aircraft. Inside the cockpit, the trainee pilot views a screen showing a computer-controlled projection of the view from a real aircraft, and makes appropriate adjustments to the controls. The computer monitors these adjustments, changes the alignment of the cockpit on its hydraulic legs, and also changes the projected view seen by the pilot. In this way a trainee pilot can progress to quite an advanced stage of training without leaving the ground.

**flip-flop** alternative name for a ▷bistable circuit.

**floating-point notation** system in which numbers are represented by means of a decimal fraction and an exponent. For example, 123,000,000,000 would be represented as 0.123 (the fraction, or mantissa) and 12 (the exponent). The exponent is the power of 10 by which the fraction must be multiplied in order to obtain the true value of the number. In other words, 123,000,000,000 can be represented by $0.123 \times 10^{12}$. Floating-point notation enables programs to work with very large and very small numbers using only a few digits; however, it is a slower system than ▷fixed-point notation and suffers from small rounding errors.

In a computer, numbers expressed in floating-point

*floppy disc*

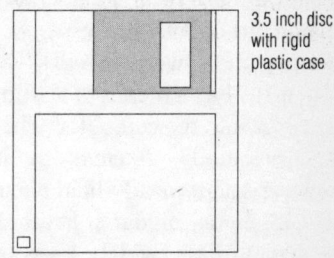

3.5 inch disc with rigid plastic case

5.25 inch disc with flexible card or plastic case

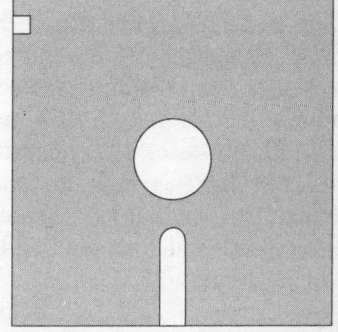

notation are represented as pairs—for example, 97.8 as (.978, +2) or .978 E2. Decimal numbers are, of course, automatically converted by the computer into ▷binary number code before storage and processing.

**floppy disc** a storage device consisting of a light, flexible disc enclosed in a cardboard or plastic jacket. The disc is placed in a disc drive, where it rotates at high speed. Data are recorded magnetically on one or both surfaces.

Floppy discs were invented by IBM in 1971 as a means of loading programs into the computer. They were originally 20 cm/8 in in diameter and typically held about 240 ◊kilobytes of data. Present-day floppy discs, widely used on ◊microcomputers, are usually either 13.13 cm/5.25 in or 8.8 cm/3.5 in in diameter, and generally hold 0.5–2 ◊megabytes, depending on the disc size, recording method, and whether one or both sides are used. Floppy discs are inexpensive, and light enough to send through the post, but have slower access speeds and are more fragile than hard discs.

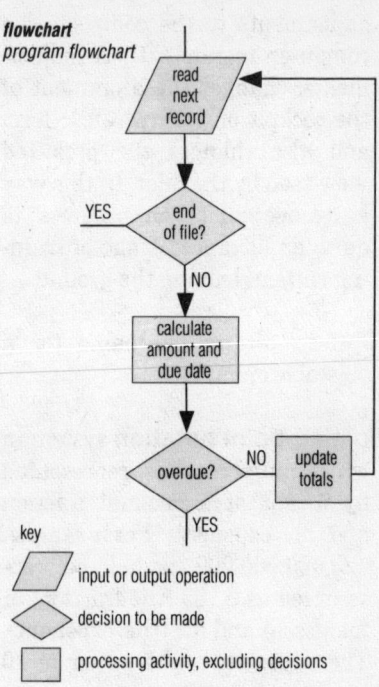

*flowchart*
program flowchart

**flow chart** diagram often used in computing to show the possible paths that data can take through a system or program.

A *system flow chart*, or *data flow chart*, is used to describe the flow of data through a complete data-processing system. Different graphic symbols represent the clerical operations involved and the different input, storage, and output equipment required. Although the flow chart may indicate the specific programs used, no details are given of how the programs process the data.

A *program flow chart* is used to describe the flow of data through a particular computer program, showing the exact sequence of operations performed by that program in order to process the data. Different graphic symbols are used to represent data input and output, decisions, branches, and ◊subroutines.

*flowchart*
system flowchart

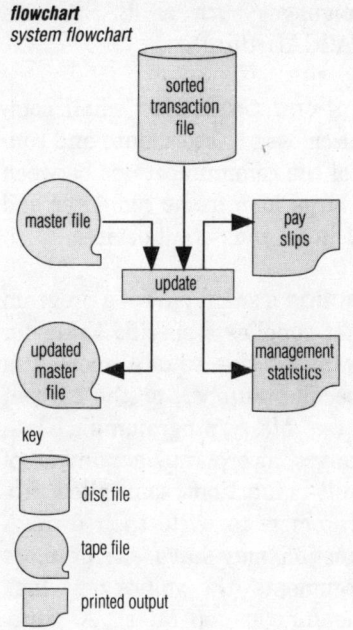

**formatting** see ◊disc formatting.

**FORTRAN** (acronym for *for*mula *tran*slation) high-level programming language best suited to mathematical and scientific computations. Developed in the mid-1950s, it is one of the earliest languages. ◊BASIC was strongly influenced by FORTRAN and is similar in many ways.

**font** complete set of printed or display characters of the same type-

*font*
common fonts

```
This is Courier 10 point.
```
**This is Times bold 12 point.**

***This is Helvetica bold italic 14 point.***

face, size, and style (bold, italic, underlined, and so on). In the UK, font sizes are measured in points, a point being approximately equivalent to 0.3 mm.

Fonts used in computer setting are of two main types: bit-mapped and outline. ***Bit-mapped fonts*** are stored in the computer memory as the exact arrangement of ◊pixels or printed dots required to produce the characters in a particular size on a screen or printer. ***Outline fonts*** are stored in the computer memory as a set of instructions for drawing the circles, straight lines, and curves that make up the outline of each character. They require a powerful computer because each character is separately generated from a set of instructions and this requires considerable computation.

Bit-mapped fonts become very ragged in appearance if they are enlarged and so a separate set of bit maps is required for each font size. In contrast, outline fonts can be scaled to any size and still maintain exactly the same appearance.

**fourth-generation language** a type of programming language designed for the rapid writing of ◊applications programs but often lacking the ability to control the individual parts of the computer. Such a language typically provides easy ways of designing screens and reports, and of using databases. Other 'generations' (the term implies a class of language rather than a chronological sequence) are ◊machine code (first generation); ◊assembly codes, or low-level languages (second); and conventional ◊high-level languages such as BASIC and PASCAL (third).

**front-end processor** small computer used to coordinate and control the communications between a large mainframe computer and its input and output devices.

**function** a small part of a program that supplies a specific value—for example, the square root of a specified number, or the current date. Most programming languages incorporate a number of built-in functions; some allow programmers to write their own. A function may have one or more arguments (the values on which the function operates). A *function key* on a keyboard is one that, when pressed, performs a designated task, such as ending a program.

**gate** in electronics, short for ◊logic gate.

**generation** stage of development in computer electronics (see ◊computer generation); a class of programming language (see ◊fourth-generation language); or a version of a file (see ◊file updating).

**gigabyte** a measure of ◊memory capacity, equal to 1,024 ◊megabytes. It is also used, less precisely, to mean 1,000 million ◊bytes.

**GIGO** (acronym for *g*arbage *i*n, *g*arbage *o*ut) expression used in computing to emphasize that inaccurate input data will result in inaccurate output data.

**global variable** a ◊variable that can be accessed by any program instruction.

**grandfather-father-son system** method of providing ◊data security by storing the three most recent versions of a master file, called the ***grandfather, father, and son*** generations of the file.

**graphical user interface** (GUI) or ***WIMP*** (*w*indows, *i*cons, *m*enus, *p*ointing device) a type of ◊user interface in which programs and files appear as icons (small pictures), user options are selected from pull-down menus, and data are displayed in windows (rectangular areas), which the operator can manipulate in various ways. The operator uses a pointing device, typically a ◊mouse, to make selections and initiate actions.

The concept of the graphical user interface was developed by the Xerox Corporation in the 1970s, was popularized with the Apple Macintosh computers in the 1980s, and is now available on many types of computer—most notably as Windows, an operating system for IBM microcomputers developed by Microsoft.

*graphical user interface*

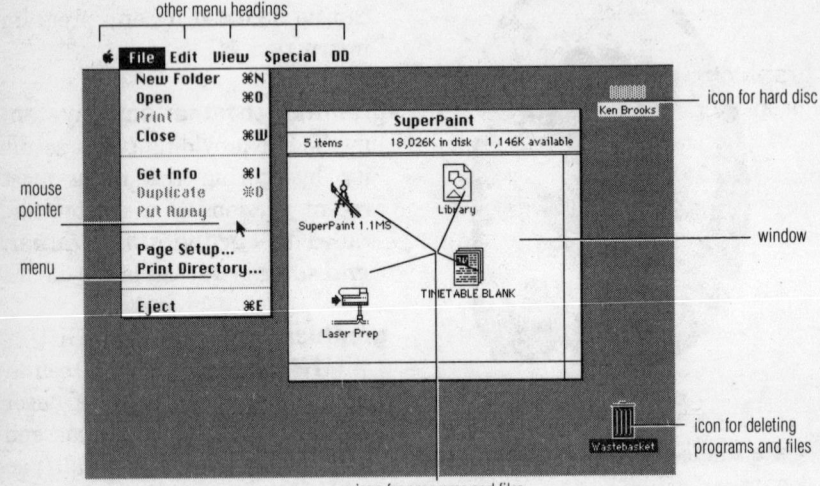

**graphics** see ⃝computer graphics.

**graphics tablet** or *bit pad* an input device in which a stylus or cursor is moved, by hand, over a flat surface. The computer can keep track of the position of the stylus, so enabling the operator to input drawings or diagrams into the computer.

A graphics tablet is often used with a form overlaid for users to mark boxes in positions that relate to specific registers in the computer. Recent developments in handwriting recognition may

*graphics tablet*

increase the future versatility of the graphics tablet.

**graph plotter** alternative name for a ▷plotter.

**GUI** abbreviation for ▷*graphical user interface*.

**hacking** unauthorized access to a computer, either for fun or for malicious or fraudulent purposes. Hackers generally use microcomputers and telephone lines to obtain access. In a wider sense the term means using software for enjoyment or self-education, not necessarily involving unauthorized access. See also ◊virus.

**handshake** an exchange of signals between two devices establishing the communications channels and protocols necessary for the devices to send and receive data.

**hard copy** computer output printed on paper to form a permanent record.

**hard disc** a storage device consisting of a rigid metal ◊disc coated with a magnetic material. Data are read from and written to the disc by means of a disc drive.

The hard disc may be permanently fixed into the drive or in the form of a disc pack that can be removed and exchanged with a different pack.

Hard discs vary from large units with capacities of over 3,000 megabytes, intended for use with mainframe computers, to small units with capacities as low as 20 megabytes, intended for use with microcomputers.

**hard-sectored disc** hard disc that is sold already formatted, so that ◊disc formatting is not necessary prior to use.

**hardware** the mechanical, electrical, and electronic components of a computer system, as opposed to the various programs, which constitute ◊software.

Hardware associated with a microcomputer might include the power supply and housing of its central processing unit, its circuit boards, visual display unit (screen), disc drive, keyboard, and printer.

**hash total** a ◊validation check in which an otherwise meaningless control total is calculated by adding together numbers (such as payroll or account numbers) associated with a set of records. The hash total is checked each time data are input, in order to ensure that no entry errors have been made.

**hertz** unit (symbol Hz) of frequency (the number of times a regular occurrence takes place in one second). The ◊clock rate of a computer is usually measured in megahertz (MHz), or millions of hertz.

**heuristics** a process by which a program attempts to improve its performance by learning from its own experience.

**hexadecimal number system** or *hex* number system to the base 16, used in computing. Normal decimal, or base-ten, numbers may be considered to be written under column headings based on the number ten. For example, the decimal number 367 stands for:

| *100s* | *10s* | *1s* |
|---|---|---|
| $(10^2)$ | $(10^1)$ | $(10^0)$ |
| 3 | 6 | 7 |

Hexadecimal numbers may be considered to be written under column headings based on the number 16. For example, the hexadecimal number 367 stands for:

| *256s* | *16s* | *1s* |
|---|---|---|
| $(16^2)$ | $(16^1)$ | $(16^0)$ |
| 3 | 6 | 7 |

The hexadecimal number 367 is therefore equivalent to the decimal number 871, since $(3 \times 256) + (6 \times 16) + (7 \times 1) = 871$.

Because only one digit or symbol can be entered in each column, in the hexadecimal system the decimal numbers 10, 11, 12, 13, 14, and 15 are represented by the letters A, B, C, D, E, and F, respectively. The hexadecimal number A3D therefore represents $(10 \times 256) + (3 \times 16) + (13 \times 1)$, or 2,621 in base 10.

Hexadecimal numbers are often preferred by programmers who write in low-level languages because they are more easily converted to the computer's internal ◊binary (base-two) code than are decimal numbers, and because they are more compact than binary numbers and therefore more easily keyed, checked, and memorized.

**high-level language** a programming language designed to suit the requirements of the programmer; it is independent of the internal machine code of any particular computer.

High-level languages are used to solve problems and are often described as ***problem-oriented languages***—for example, BASIC was designed to be easily learnt by first-time programmers; COBOL is used to write programs solving business problems; and FORTRAN is used for programs solving scientific and mathematical problems. In contrast, low-level languages, such as ◊assembly languages, closely reflect the machine codes of specific computers, and are therefore described as ***machine-oriented languages***.

Unlike low-level languages, high-level languages are relatively easy to learn because the instructions bear a close resemblance to everyday language, and the programmer does not require detailed knowledge of the internal workings of the computer.

Each instruction in a high-level language is equivalent to several machine-code instructions. High-level programs are therefore more compact than equivalent low-level programs. However, each high-level instruction must be translated into machine code—by either a ◊compiler or an ◊interpreter program—before it can be executed by a computer.

High-level languages are designed to be ***portable***—programs written in a high-level language can be run on any computer that has a compiler or interpreter for that particular language.

**Hypertext** system for viewing information (both text and pictures) on a computer screen in such a way that related items of information can easily be reached. For example, the program might display a map of a country; if the user clicks (with a ◊mouse) on a particular city, the program will display some information about that city.

**IBM** (abbreviation for *International Business Machines*) multinational company, the largest manufacturer of computers in the world. The company is a descendant of the Tabulating Machine Company, formed 1896 by US scientist Herman Hollerith (1860–1929) to exploit his punched-card machines. It adopted its present name in 1924. By 1991 it had an annual turnover of $64.8 billion and employed about 345,000 people.

**icon** a small picture on the computer screen, or ◊visual display unit (VDU), representing an object or function that the user may manipulate or otherwise use. It is a feature of ◊graphical user-interface (GUI) systems. Icons make computers easier to use by allowing the user to point to and click with a ◊mouse on pictures, rather than type commands.

**immediate-access memory** ◊memory provided in the ◊central processing unit to store the programs and data in current use.

**impact printer** computer printer that creates characters by striking an inked ribbon against the paper beneath. Examples of impact printers are dot-matrix printers, daisywheel printers, and most types of line printer.

Impact printers are noisier and slower than non-impact printers, such as ink-jet and laser printers, but they can be used to produce carbon copies.

**import file** a file that can be read by a program even though it was produced as an ◊export file by a different program or by a different make of computer.

**indexed sequential file** a type of ◊file access in which an index is used to obtain the address of the

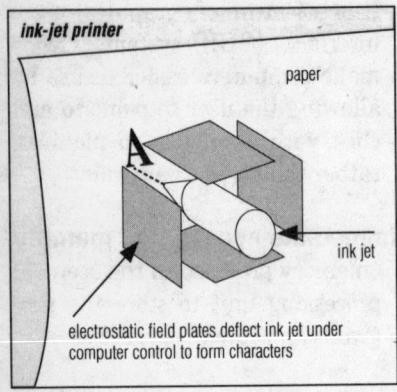
*ink-jet printer*

paper
ink jet
electrostatic field plates deflect ink jet under computer control to form characters

◊block containing the required record.

**information technology** collective term for the various technologies involved in processing and transmitting information. They include computing, telecommunications, and microelectronics.

**ink-jet printer** computer printer that creates characters and graphics by spraying very fine jets of quick-drying ink onto paper. Ink-jet printers range in size from small machines designed to work with microcomputers to very large machines designed for high-volume commercial printing.

Because they produce high-quality printing and are virtually silent, small ink-jet printers (along with ◊laser printers) are beginning to replace impact printers, such as dot-matrix and daisywheel printers, for use with microcomputers.

**input device** device for entering information into a computer. Input devices include keyboards, joysticks, mice, light pens, touch-sensitive screens, graphics tablets, speech-recognition devices, and vision systems. Compare ◊output device.

Input devices that are used commercially—for example, by banks, postal services, and supermarkets—must be able to read and capture large volumes of data very rapidly. Such devices include document readers for magnetic-ink character recognition (MICR), optical character recognition (OCR), and optical mark recognition (OMR); magnetic-strip readers; mark-sense readers; bar-code scanners; and point-of-sale (POS) terminals. Punched-card and paper-tape readers were used in earlier commercial applications but are now obsolete.

**instruction register** a special memory location used to hold the instruction that the computer is currently processing. It is located in the control unit of the ◊central processing unit, and receives instructions individually from the immediate-access memory during the fetch phase of the ◊fetch–execute cycle.

**instruction set** the complete set of machine-code instructions that a computer's central processing unit can obey.

**integrated circuit** (IC), popularly called *silicon chip*, a miniaturized electronic circuit produced on a single crystal, or chip, of a semiconducting material—usually silicon. It may contain many thousands of components and yet measure only 5 mm square and 1 mm thick.

The IC is encapsulated within a plastic or ceramic case, and linked via gold wires to metal pins with which it is connected to a ◊printed circuit board and the other components that make up such electronic devices as computers and calculators.

**integrated services digital network** (ISDN) internationally developed telecommunications system for sending signals in

*integrated circuit*

*the packaging of a silicon 'chip'*

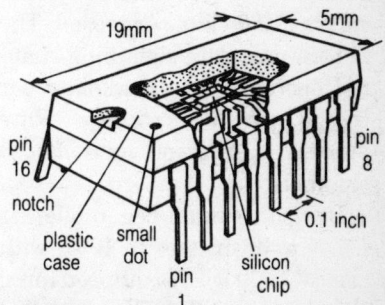

◊digital format along optical fibres and coaxial cable. It involves converting the 'local loop'—the link between the user's telephone (or private automatic branch exchange) and the digital telephone exchange—from an ◊analogue system into a digital system, thereby greatly increasing the amount of information that can be carried. The first large-scale use of ISDN began in Japan in 1988.

ISDN has advantages in higher voice quality, better-quality faxes, and the possibility of data transfer between computers six times faster than current modems. With ISDN's *Basic Rate Access*, a multiplexer divides one voice telephone line into three channels: two B bands and a D band. Each B band offers 64 kilobits per second and can carry one voice conversation or 50 simultaneous data calls at 1,200 bits per second. The D band is a data-signalling channel operating at 16 kilobits per second. With *Primary Rate Access*, ISDN provides 30 B channels.

British Telecom began offering ISDN to businesses in 1991, with some 47,000 ISDN-equipped lines. Its adoption in the UK is expected to stimulate the use of data-communications services such as faxing, teleshopping, and home banking.

New services may include computer conferencing, where both voice and computer communications take place simultaneously, and videophones.

**intelligent terminal** a ◊terminal with its own processor which can, if necessary, take some of the processing load away from the main computer.

**interactive computing** a system for processing data in which the operator is in direct communication with the computer, receiving immediate responses to input data. In ◊batch processing, by contrast, the necessary data and instructions are prepared in advance and processed by the computer with little or no intervention from the operator.

*interface*

*the back of a typical microcomputer showing range of interfaces provided*

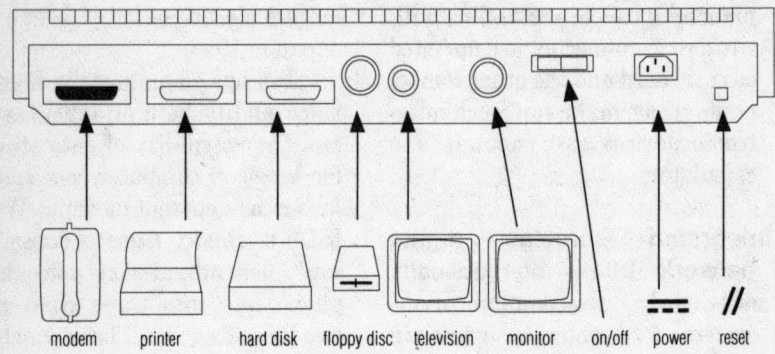

**interactive video** (IV) computer-mediated system that enables the user to interact with and control information (including text, recorded speech, or moving images) stored on video disc. IV is most commonly used for training purposes, using analogue video discs, but has wider applications with digital video systems such as CD-I (Compact Disc Interactive, from Philips and Sony) and DVI (Digital Video Interactive, from Intel).

**interface** the point of contact between two programs or pieces of equipment. The term is most often used for the physical connection between the computer and a ◊peripheral device, which is used to compensate for differences in such operating characteristics as speed, data coding, voltage, and power consumption. For example, a *printer interface* is the cabling and circuitry used to transfer data from a computer to a printer, and to compensate for differences in speed and coding.

Common standard interfaces include the ◊*Centronics interface*, used to connect ◊parallel devices, and the ◊*RS232 interface*, used to connect ◊serial devices. For example, in many microcomputer systems, an RS232 interface is used to connect the microcomputer to a modem, and a Centronics device is used to connect it to a printer.

**interpreter** computer program that translates and executes a program written in a high-level language. Unlike a ◊compiler, which produces a complete machine-code translation of the high-level program in one operation, an interpreter translates the source program, instruction

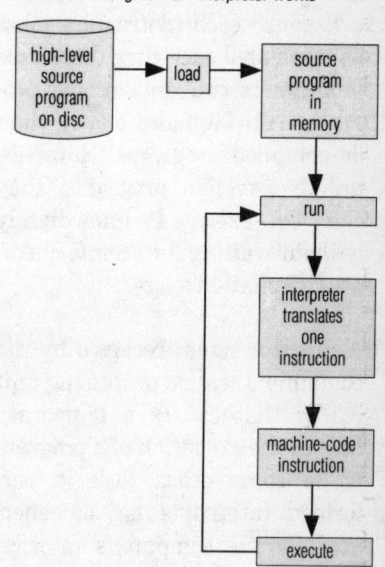

*interpreter*

flowchart showing how an interpreter works

by instruction, each time that program is run.

Because each instruction must be translated each time the source program is run, interpreted programs run far more slowly than do compiled programs. However, unlike compiled programs, they can be executed immediately without waiting for an intermediate compilation stage.

**interrupt** a signal received by the computer's central processing unit (CPU) that causes a temporary halt in the execution of a program while some other task is performed. Interrupts may be generated by the computer's internal electronic clock (clock interrupt), by an input or output device, or by a software routine. After the computer has completed the task to which it was diverted, control returns to the original program.

For example, many computers, while printing a long document, allow the user to carry on with other work. When the printer is ready for more data, it sends an interrupt signal that causes the computer to halt work on the user's program and transmit more data to the printer.

**inverse video** or *reverse video* a display mode in which images on a display screen are presented as a negative of their normal appearance. For example, if the computer screen normally displays dark images on a light background, inverse video will change all or part of the screen to a light image on a dark background.

Inverse video is commonly used to highlight parts of a display or to mark out text and pictures that the user wishes the computer to change in some way. For example, the user of a word-processing program might use a pointing device such as a ◊mouse to mark in inverse video a paragraph of text that is to be deleted from the document.

**inverted file** a file that reorganizes the structure of an existing data file to enable a rapid search to be made for all records having one field falling within set limits.

For example, a file used by an estate agent might store records on each house for sale, using a reference number as the key field for ◊sorting. One field in each record would be the asking price of the house. To speed up the process of drawing up lists of houses falling within certain price ranges, an inverted file might be created in which the records are rearranged according to price. Each record would consist of an asking price, followed by the reference numbers of all the houses offered for sale at this approximate price.

**ISBN** (abbreviation for *International Standard Book Number*) code number used for ordering or classifying book titles. The final digit in each ISBN number is a check digit, which can be used by a computer program to validate the number each time it is input (see ◊validation).

**ISDN** abbreviation for ◊*integrated services digital network*, a telecommunications system.

**iteration** a method of solving a problem by performing the same steps repeatedly until a certain condition is satisfied. For example, in one method of ◊sorting, adjacent items are repeatedly exchanged until the data are in the required sequence.

**joystick** an input device that signals to a computer the direction and extent of displacement of a hand-held lever. It is similar to the joystick used to control the flight of an aircraft. Joysticks are sometimes used to control the movement of a cursor (marker) across a display screen, but are much more frequently used to provide fast and direct input for moving the characters and symbols that feature in computer games. Unlike a ◊mouse, which can move a pointer in any direction, simple games joysticks are often only capable of moving an object in one of eight different directions.

*joystick*

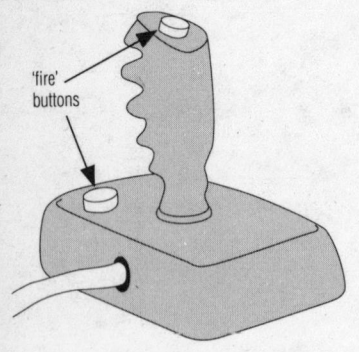

'fire' buttons

**jump** a programming instruction that causes the computer to branch to a different part of a program, rather than execute the next instruction in the program sequence. Unconditional jumps are always executed; conditional jumps are only executed if a particular condition is satisfied.

**justification** in printing and word processing, the arrangement of text so that it is aligned with either the left or right margin, or both.
*Left-justified text* has lines of different length that are perfectly aligned with the left margin but not with the right margin. The left margin is straight but the right margin is uneven, or ragged.
*Right-justified text*, normally only used for columns of numbers,

has lines of different length that are perfectly aligned with the right margin but not with the left margin. The right margin is straight but the left margin is ragged.

***Fully justified text*** has lines of the same length that are perfectly aligned with both the left and the right margins. Both margins are even. Many word processors can automatically produce fully justified text by inserting extra spaces between the words in each line, or by adjusting the spacing between the letters (microspacing).

---

*justification*

This is an example of text that is left justified. The lines are of unequal length and are aligned with the left margin

This is an example of text that is right justified. The lines are of unequal length and are aligned with the right margin

This is an example of text that is fully justified. The lines are of equal length and are aligned with both the left and the right margins.

**keyboard** an input device resembling a typewriter keyboard, used to enter instructions and data. There are many variations on the layout and labelling of keys. Extra numeric keys may be added, as may special-purpose function keys, whose effects can be defined by programs in the computer.

**key field** selected field, or portion, of a record that is used to identify that record uniquely; in a file of records it is the field used as the basis for ▷sorting the file. For example, in a file containing details of a bank's customers, the customer account number would probably be used as the key field.

**key-to-disc system** or *key-to-tape system* a system that enables large amounts of data to be entered at a keyboard and trans-

*keyboard*
typical computer keyboard

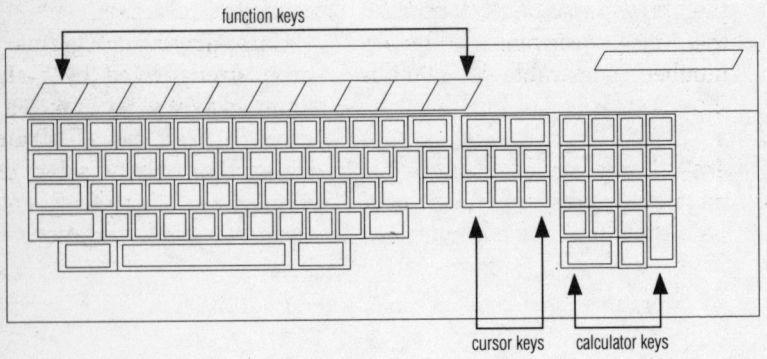

ferred directly onto computer-readable discs or tapes.

Such systems are used in ◊batch processing, in which batches of data, prepared in advance, are processed by computer with little or no intervention from the user. The preparation of the data may be controlled by a minicomputer, freeing a larger, mainframe computer for the task of processing.

**kilobyte** (K or Kb) a unit of memory equal to 1,024 ◊bytes. It is sometimes used, less precisely, to mean 1,000 bytes.

In the metric system, the prefix 'kilo-' denotes multiplication by 1,000 (as in kilometre, a unit equal to 1,000 metres). However, computer memory size is based on the ◊binary number system, and the most convenient binary number comparable to 1,000 is $2^{10}$, or 1,024.

**Kimball tag** stock-control device commonly used in clothes shops, consisting of a small ◊punched card attached to each item offered for sale. The tag carries information about the item (such as its serial number, price, colour, and size), both in the form of printed details (which can be read by the customer) and as a pattern of small holes. When the item is sold, the tag (or a part of the tag) is removed and kept as a computer-readable record of sales.

**knowledge-based system** (KBS) computer program that uses an encoding of human knowledge to help solve problems. It was discovered, during research into ◊artificial intelligence, that adding heuristics (rules of thumb) enabled programs to tackle problems that were otherwise difficult to solve by the usual techniques of computer science.

Chess-playing programs have been strengthened by including knowledge of what makes a good position, or of overall strategies, rather than relying solely on the computer's ability to calculate the range of possible variations.

**LAN** acronym for ◊*local area network*.

**laptop computer** portable microcomputer, small enough to be used on the operator's lap. It comprises a single unit, incorporating a keyboard, floppy or hard disc drives, and a screen. The screen often forms a lid that folds back in use. It uses a liquid-crystal or gas-plasma display, rather than the bulkier and heavier cathode-ray tubes found in most display terminals. A typical laptop computer measures about 360 × 380 × 100 mm, and weighs between 3 and 7 kg.

**laser printer** computer printer in which the image to be printed is formed by the action of a laser on a light-sensitive drum, then transferred to paper by means of an electrostatic charge. Laser printers are page printers, printing a complete page at a time. The printed image, which can take the form of text or pictures, is made up of tiny dots, or ink particles. The quality of the image generated depends on the fineness of these dots—most laser printers can print up to 120 dots per cm/ 300 dots per in across the page.

A typical desktop laser printer can print about 4 to 20 pages per minute. The first low-cost laser printer suitable for office use appeared in 1984.

Laser printers range in size from small machines designed to work with microcomputers to very large machines designed for high-volume commercial printing. Because they produce very high-quality print and are virtually silent, small laser printers (along with ◊ink-jet printers) have replaced ◊dot-matrix and ◊daisy-wheel printers as the most popular type of microcomputer printer.

**LCD** abbreviation for ◊*liquid-crystal display*.

**LED** abbreviation for ◊*light-emitting diode*.

**library program** one of a collection, or library, of regularly used software routines, held in a computer backing store. For example, a programmer might store a routine for sorting a file into ◊key field order, and so could incorporate it easily into any new program being developed instead of having to rewrite it.

**light-emitting diode** (LED) means of displaying symbols in electronic instruments and devices. An LED is made of ◊semiconductor material, such as gallium arsenide phosphide, that glows when electricity is passed through it. The first digital watches and calculators had LED displays, but many later models use ◊liquid-crystal displays.

**light pen** a device resembling an ordinary pen, used to indicate locations on a computer screen.

With certain computer-aided design (◊CAD) programs, the light pen can be used to instruct the computer to change the shape, size, position, and colours of sections of a screen image.

*light pen*

The pen has a photoreceptor at its tip that emits signals when light from the screen passes beneath it. From the timing of this signal and a gridlike representation of the screen in the computer memory, a computer program can calculate the position of the light pen.

**line printer** computer ◊printer that prints a complete line of characters at a time. Line printers can achieve very high printing speeds of up to 2,500 lines a minute, but can print in only one typeface, cannot print graphics, and are very noisy. Until the late 1980s they were the obvious choice for high-volume printing, but high-speed ◊page printers, such as laser printers, are now preferred.

**liquid-crystal display** (LCD) display of numbers (for example, in a calculator) or pictures (such as on a pocket television screen) produced by molecules of a substance in a semiliquid state with some crystalline properties, so that clusters of molecules align in parallel formations. The display is a blank until the application of an electric field, which 'twists' the molecules so that they reflect or transmit light falling on them.

**LISP** (acronym for *list p*rocessing) high-level programming language designed for manipulating lists of data items. It is used primarily in research into ◊artificial intelligence (AI). Developed in the 1960s, and until recently common only in university laboratories, LISP is used more in the USA than in Europe, where the language ◊PROLOG is often preferred for AI work.

**local area network** (LAN) a ◊network restricted to a single room or building. Local area networks enable up to 500 devices to be connected together.

**local variable** a ◊variable that can be accessed only by following the instructions within a particular ◊subroutine.

**logical error** an ◊error in the program's design. A logical error may cause a program to fail to respond in the correct way to user requests or to crash completely.

**logic gate** or *logic circuit* in electronics, one of the basic components used in the building of ◊integrated circuits. The five basic types of gate make logical decisions based on the functions NOT, AND, OR, NAND (NOT AND), and NOR (NOT OR). With the exception of the NOT gate, each has two or more inputs.

Information is fed to a gate in the form of binary-coded input signals (logic value 0 stands for 'off' or 'low-voltage pulse', logic 1 for 'on' or 'high-voltage'), and each combination of input signals yields a specific output (logic 0 or 1). An *OR* gate will give a logic 1 output if one or more of its inputs receives a logic 1 signal; however, an *AND* gate will yield a logic 1 output only if it receives a logic 1 signal through both its inputs. The output of a *NOT* or *inverter* gate is the opposite of the signal

## logic gate
*circuit symbols*

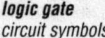

OR gate  AND gate  NOT or inverter gate  NOR gate  NAND gate

*truth tables*

| inputs | | output |
|---|---|---|
| 0 | 0 | 0 |
| 0 | 1 | 1 |
| 1 | 0 | 1 |
| 1 | 1 | 1 |

OR gate

| inputs | | output |
|---|---|---|
| 0 | 0 | 0 |
| 0 | 1 | 0 |
| 1 | 0 | 0 |
| 1 | 1 | 1 |

AND gate

| inputs | output |
|---|---|
| 0 | 1 |
| 1 | 0 |

NOT gate

| inputs | | output |
|---|---|---|
| 0 | 0 | 1 |
| 0 | 1 | 0 |
| 1 | 0 | 0 |
| 1 | 1 | 0 |

NOR gate

| inputs | | output |
|---|---|---|
| 0 | 0 | 1 |
| 0 | 1 | 1 |
| 1 | 0 | 1 |
| 1 | 1 | 0 |

NAND gate

received through its single input, and a ***NOR*** or ***NAND*** gate produces an output signal that is the opposite of the signal that would have been produced by an OR or AND gate respectively. The properties of a logic gate, or of a combination of gates, may be defined and presented in the form of a diagram called a ***truth table***, which lists the output that will be triggered by each of the possible combinations of input signals.

**LOGO** (Greek *logos* 'word') high-level programming language designed to teach mathematical concepts. Developed about 1970 at the Massachusetts Institute of Technology, it became popular in schools and with home computer users because of its 'turtle graphics' feature. This allows the user to write programs that create line drawings on a computer screen, or drive a small mobile robot (a 'turtle' or 'buggy') around the floor. LOGO encourages the logical and structured use of languages, leading to 'microworlds', in which problems can be solved by using a few standard solutions.

**log off** or ***log out*** the process by which a user identifies himself or herself to a multiuser computer and leaves the system.

**log on** or ***log in*** the process by which a user identifies himself or

**loop**

herself to a multiuser computer and enters the system. Logging on may require the user to enter a password before access is allowed.

**loop** short for ◊program loop.

**Lotus 1–2–3** ◊spreadsheet computer program, produced by Lotus Development Corporation. It first appeared in 1982 and its combination of spreadsheet, graphics display, and data management contributed to the rapid acceptance of the IBM Personal Computer in businesses.

**low-level language** a programming language designed for a particular computer and reflecting its internal ◊machine code; low-level languages are therefore often described as *machine-oriented* languages. They cannot easily be converted to run on a computer with a different central processing unit, and they are relatively difficult to learn because a detailed knowledge of the internal working of the computer is required. Since they must be translated into machine code by an ◊assembler program, low-level languages are also called ◊assembly languages.

A mnemonic-based low-level language can replace binary machine-code instructions, which are very hard to remember, write down, or correct, with short codes chosen to remind the programmer of the instructions they represent. For example, the binary-code instruction that means '*st*ore the contents of the *a*ccumulator' may be represented with the mnemonic STA.

**LSI** (abbreviation for *large-scale integration*) the technology that enables whole electrical circuits to be etched into a piece of semiconducting material just a few millimetres square.

By the late 1960s a complete computer processor could be incorporated on a single chip, or ◊integrated circuit, and in 1971 the US electronics company Intel produced the first commercially available ◊microprocessor. Very large-scale integration (◊VLSI) results in even smaller chips.

**machine code** a set of instructions that a computer's central processing unit (CPU) can understand and obey directly, without any translation. Each type of CPU has its own machine code. Because machine-code programs consist entirely of binary digits (bits), the process of writing and checking such programs is very slow and laborious. Most programmers therefore do not use machine code directly but write their programs in an easy-to-use ◊high-level language. A high-level program must be translated into machine code—by means of a ◊compiler or ◊interpreter program—before it can be executed by a computer.

Where no suitable high-level language exists or where very efficient machine code is required, programmers may choose to write programs in a low-level, or assembly, language, which can be eventually translated into machine code by means of an ◊assembler program.

Microprocessors (CPUs based on a single integrated circuit) may be classified according to the number of machine-code instructions that they are capable of obeying: ◊CISC (complex instruction set computer) microprocessors can support up to 200 instructions, whereas ◊RISC (reduced instruction set computer) microprocessors support far fewer instructions but execute programs more rapidly.

**Macintosh** range of microcomputers produced by Apple Computers. The Apple Macintosh, introduced in 1984, was the first popular microcomputer with a ◊graphical user interface (GUI).

The success of the Macintosh prompted other manufacturers and software companies to create their own GUIs. Most notable of these are *Presentation Manager*, which is part of the IBM

OS/2 operating system, and *Windows*, which was produced for IBM microcomputers by the software company Microsoft.

**macro** in programming, a new command created by combining a number of existing ones. For example, if a programming language has separate commands for obtaining data from the keyboard and for displaying data on the screen, the programmer might create a macro that performs both these tasks with one command. A *macro key* on the keyboard combines the effects of pressing several individual keys.

**magnetic-ink character recognition** (MICR) a technique that enables special characters printed in magnetic ink to be read and input rapidly to a computer. MICR is used extensively in banking because magnetic-ink characters are difficult to forge and are therefore ideal for marking and identifying cheques.

**magnetic strip** or *magnetic stripe* thin strip of magnetic material attached to a plastic card (such as a credit card) and used for recording data.

**magnetic tape** narrow plastic ribbon coated with an easily magnetizable material on which data can be recorded. It is used in sound recording, audiovisual systems (videotape), and computing. For mass storage on commercial mainframe computers, large reel-to-reel tapes are used, but for the smaller mini- and microcomputers, tape cassettes and cartridges are more usual.

Magnetic tape was first used to record computer data and programs in 1951 as part of the UNIVAC 1 system. It was very popular as a storage medium for external memory in the 1950s and 1960s. Since then it has been largely replaced by magnetic ◊discs as a working medium, although tape is still used to make backup copies of important data. Information is recorded on the tape in binary form, with two different strengths of signal representing 1 and 0. It is common for 20,000 ◊bits of information to be recorded on each centimetre of tape. The tape drive of a mainframe or minicomputer may be able to read 5 m of tape in a second.

**mail merge** a feature offered by some word-processing packages

***magnetic-ink character recognition***
MICR

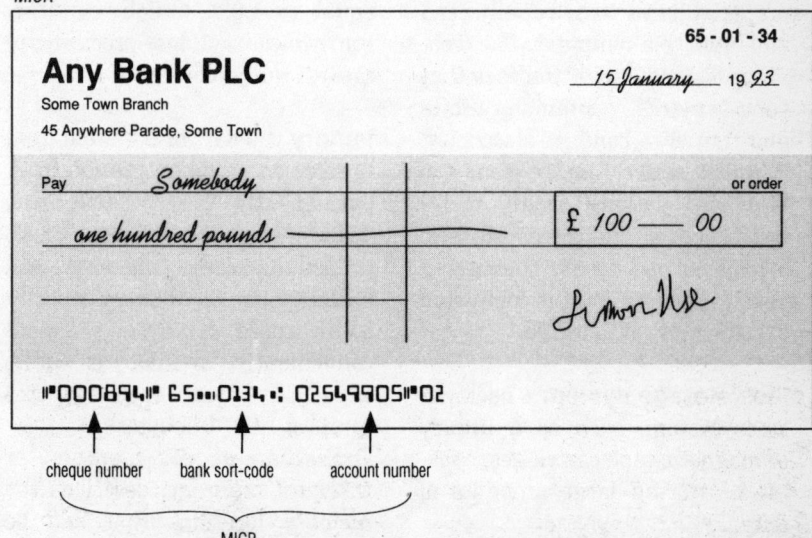

that enables a list of personal details, such as names and addresses, to be combined with a general document outline to produce individualized documents. For example, a club secretary might create a file containing a mailing list of the names and addresses of the club members. Whenever a letter is to be sent to all club members, a general letter outline is prepared with indications as to where individual names and addresses need be added. The mail merge combines the file of names and addresses with the letter outline to produce individual letters addressed to each club member.

**mainframe** large computer used for commercial data processing and other large-scale operations. Because of the general increase in computing power, the differences between the mainframe, ◊supercomputer, ◊minicomputer, and ◊microcomputer (personal computer) are becoming less marked.

**mark sensing** a technique that enables pencil marks made in predetermined positions on specially prepared forms to be rapidly read and input to a computer. The technique makes use of the fact that pencil marks contain graphite and therefore conduct electricity. A *mark sense reader* scans the form by passing small metal brushes over the paper surface. Whenever a brush touches a pencil mark a circuit is completed and the mark is detected.

**mass storage system** a backing-store system, such as a library of magnetic-tape cartridges, capable of storing large amounts of data.

**master file** a file that is the main source of data for a particular application. Various methods of ◊file updating are used to ensure that the data in the master file are accurate and up to date.

**media** (singular *medium*) the collective name for materials on which data can be recorded. For example, a floppy disc is a medium for recording magnetic data.

**media librarian** alternative name for a ◊file librarian.

**megabyte** (Mb) a unit of memory equal to 1,024 ◊kilobytes. It is sometimes used, less precisely, to mean 1 million bytes.

**memory** the part of a system used to store data and programs either permanently or temporarily. There are two main types: immediate-access memory and backing storage. Memory capacity is measured in ◊bytes or, more conveniently, in kilobytes (units of 1,024 bytes) or megabytes (units of 1,024 kilobytes).

*Immediate-access memory*, or *internal memory*, describes the memory locations that can be addressed directly and individually by the central processing unit. It is either read-only (stored in ◊ROM, ◊PROM, and ◊EPROM chips) or read/write (stored in ◊RAM chips). Read-only memory stores information that must be constantly available or accessed very quickly, and is unlikely to be changed. It is non-volatile—that is, it is not lost when the computer is switched off. Read/write memory is volatile—it stores programs and data only while the computer is switched on.

*Backing storage*, or *external memory*, is non-volatile memory,

*microcomputer*

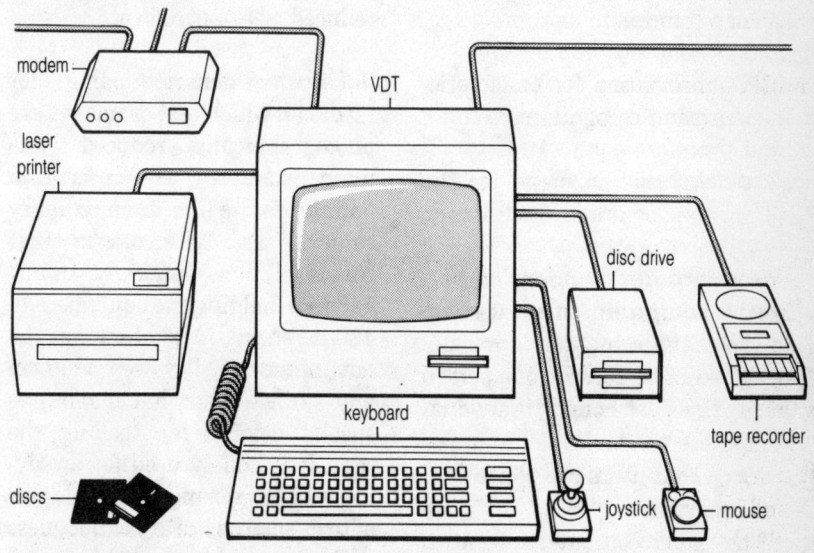

located outside the central processing unit, used to store programs and data not currently in use. Backing storage is provided by such devices as magnetic ◊discs (floppy and hard discs), ◊magnetic tape (tape streamers and cassettes), optical discs (such as ◊CD-ROM), and ◊bubble memory. By rapidly switching blocks of information between the backing storage and the immediate-access memory, the limited size of the immediate-access memory may be increased artificially. When this technique is used to give the appearance of a larger internal memory than physically exists, the additional capacity is referred to as ◊virtual memory.

**menu** a list of options, displayed on screen, from which the user may make a choice—for example, the choice of services offered to the customer by a bank cash dispenser: withdrawal, deposit, balance, or statement. Menus are used extensively in ◊graphical user-interface (GUI) systems, where the menu options are often selected using a pointing device called a ◊mouse.

**MICR** abbreviation for ◊magnetic-ink character recognition.

**microchip** popular name for the silicon chip, or ◊integrated circuit.

**microcomputer** or *micro* or *personal computer* small desktop or portable computer, typically designed to be used by one person at a time, although individual computers can be linked in a network so that users can share data and programs.

The microcomputer's central processing unit is a ◊microprocessor, contained on a single ◊integrated circuit.

Microcomputers are the smallest of the four classes of computer (the other classes are the supercomputer, mainframe, and minicomputer).

Since the appearance in 1975 of the first commercially available microcomputer, the Altair 8800, microcomputers have become widely accepted in commerce, industry, and education.

**microfiche** sheet of film on which printed text is photographically reduced. See ◊microform.

**microform** generic name for media on which text or images are photographically reduced. The main examples are *microfilm* (similar to the film in an ordinary camera) and *microfiche* (flat sheets of film, generally 105 × 148 mm, holding the equivalent of 420 A4 sheets). Microform has the advantage of low reproduction and storage costs, but it requires special devices for reading the text. It is widely used for archiving and for storing large volumes of text, such as library catalogues.

Computer data may be output directly and quickly in microform by means of COM (computer output on microfilm/microfiche) techniques.

**microprocessor** complete computer ◊central processing unit contained on a single ◊integrated circuit, or chip.

The appearance of the first microprocessors in 1971 heralded the introduction of the microcomputer. The microprocessor has led to a dramatic fall in the size and cost of computers, and ◊dedicated computers can now be found as integral parts of washing machines, cars, and so on.

**MIDI** (acronym for *m*usical *i*nstruments *d*igital *i*nterface) standard ◊interface that enables electronic musical instruments to be connected to a computer. A computer with a MIDI interface can input and store the sounds produced by the connected instruments, and can then manipulate these sounds in many different ways. For example, a single keystroke may change the key of an entire composition. Even a full written score for the composition may be automatically produced.

**minicomputer** multiuser computer with a size and processing power between those of a ◊mainframe and a ◊microcomputer.

Minicomputers are often used in medium-sized businesses and university departments handling ◊database or other commercial programs and running scientific or graphical applications requiring a great deal of numerical computation.

**mips** (acronym for *m*illion *i*nstructions *p*er *s*econd) a measure of the speed of a processor. It does not equal the computer power in all cases. The original IBM personal computer had a speed of 0.25 mips.

**mnemonic** a short sequence of letters used in low-level programming languages (see ◊low-level language) to represent a ◊machine-code instruction.

**modem** (acronym for *mo*dulator/*dem*odulator) device for transmitting computer data over telephone lines. Such a device is necessary because the ◊digital signals produced by computers cannot, at present, be transmitted directly over the telephone network, which uses ◊analogue signals. The modem converts the digital signals to analogue, and back again. Modems are used for linking remote terminals to central computers and enable computers to communicate with each other anywhere in the world.

**motherboard** ◊printed circuit board that contains the main components of a microcomputer. The power, memory capacity, and capability of the microcomputer may be enhanced by adding

*mouse*

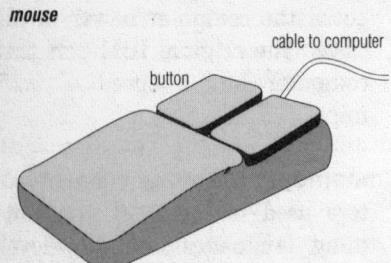

expansion boards to the motherboard.

**mouse** an input device used to control a pointer on a computer screen. It is a feature of ◊graphical user-interface (GUI) systems. The mouse is about the size of a pack of playing cards, is connected to the computer by a wire, and incorporates one or more buttons that can be pressed. Moving the mouse across a flat surface causes a corresponding movement of the pointer. In this way, the operator can manipulate objects on the screen and make menu selections.

**MS-DOS** (abbreviation for *M*icro*s*oft *D*isc *O*perating *S*ystem) computer ◊operating system produced by Microsoft Corporation, widely used on ◊microcomputers with 16-bit microprocessors. A version called PC-DOS is sold by IBM specifically for their range of personal computers. MS-DOS and PC-DOS are usually referred to as DOS. MS-DOS first appeared in the early 1980s, and was based on an earlier system for computers with 8-bit microprocessors, CP/M.

**multimedia** computer system that combines audio and video components to create an interactive application that uses text, sound, and graphics (still, animated, and video sequences). For example, a multimedia database of musical instruments may allow a user not only to search and retrieve text about a particular instrument but also to see pictures of it and hear it play a piece of music.

◊CD-ROM is frequently used as a backing storage for such systems because of its high storage capacity.

In training applications based on multimedia, the student's responses to questions displayed using pictures, text, and sound are monitored by the computer and the student's route through the training material is adjusted accordingly.

**multiplexer** in telecommunications, a device that allows a transmission medium to carry a number of separate signals at the same time—enabling, for example, several telephone conversations to be carried by one telephone line, and data from several terminals to be carried to one computer.

**multitasking** or *multiprogramming* a system in which one processor appears to run several different programs (or different parts of the same program) at the same time. All the programs are held in memory together and each is allowed to run for a certain period—for example while other programs are waiting for a ◊peripheral device to work or for input from an operator. The ability to multitask depends on the ◊operating system rather than the type of computer. Unix is one of the commonest.

**multiuser system** or *multiaccess system* an operating system that enables several users to access the same computer apparently at the same time. Each user has a terminal, which may be local (connected directly to the computer) or remote (connected to the computer via a modem and a telephone line). Multiaccess is usually achieved by *time-sharing*: the computer switches very rapidly between terminals and programs so that each user has sole use of the computer for only a fraction of a second but can work as if she or he had continuous access.

**NAND gate** a type of ◊logic gate.

**network** a method of connecting computers so that they can share data and ◊peripheral devices, such as printers. The main types are classified by the pattern of the connections—star or ring network, for example—or by the degree of geographical spread allowed; for example, local area networks (LANs) for communication within a room or building, and wide area networks (WANs) for more remote systems.

*network*
*local area network*

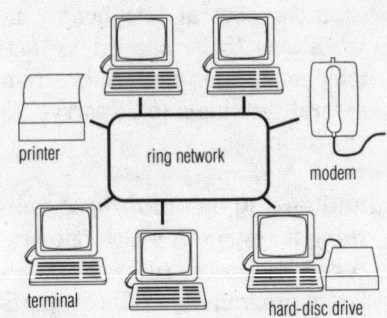

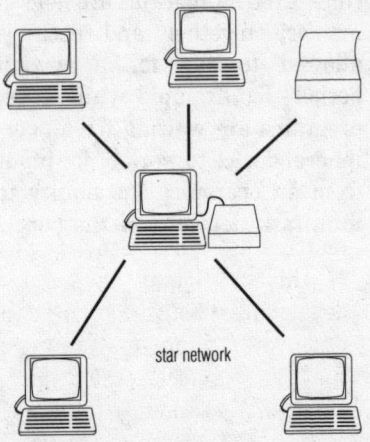

**neural network** an artificial network of processors that attempts to mimic the structure of nerve cells (neurons) in the human brain. Neural networks may be electronic, optical, or simulated by computer software.

The chief characteristic of neural networks is their ability to sum up large amounts of imprecise data and decide whether they

## notebook computer

*network*

*wide area network*

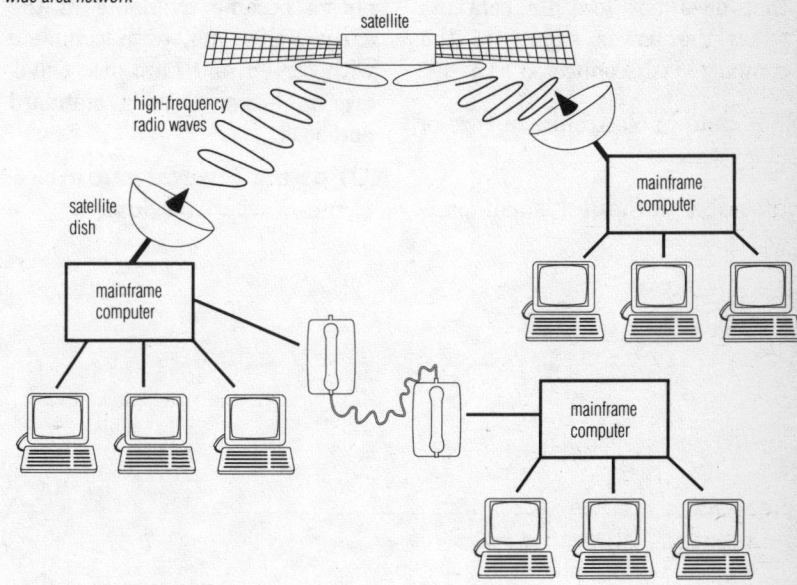

match a pattern or not. Networks of this type may be used in developing robot vision, matching fingerprints, and analysing fluctuations in stock-market prices. However, it is thought unlikely by scientists that such networks will ever be able accurately to imitate the human brain, which is very much more complicated; it contains around 10 billion nerve cells, whereas current artificial networks contain only a hundred processors or so.

*notebook computer*

**non-volatile memory** ♦memory that does not lose its contents when the power supply to the computer is disconnected.

**NOR gate** in electronics, a type of ♦logic gate.

**notebook computer** small portable computer. Notebook computers became available in the early 1990s and, even complete with screen and hard-disc drive, are no larger than a standard notebook.

**NOT gate** or *inverter gate* in electronics, a type of ♦logic gate.

**OCR** abbreviation for ◊*optical character recognition*.

**octal number system** number system to the base eight, used in computing. The highest digit that can appear in the octal system is seven. Normal decimal, or base-ten, numbers may be considered to be written under column headings based on the number ten. For example, the decimal number 567 stands for:

| *100s* | *10s* | *1s* |
|---|---|---|
| *($10^2$)* | *($10^1$)* | *($10^0$)* |
| 5 | 6 | 7 |

Octal, or base-eight, numbers can be thought of as written under column headings based on the number eight. For example, the octal number 567 stands for:

| *64s* | *8s* | *1s* |
|---|---|---|
| *($8^2$)* | *($8^1$)* | *($8^0$)* |
| 5 | 6 | 7 |

The octal number 567 is therefore equivalent to the decimal number 375, since $(5 \times 64) + (6 \times 8) + (7 \times 1) = 375$.

The octal number system is sometimes used by computer programmers as an alternative to the ◊hexadecimal number system.

**object-oriented programming** (OOP) computer programming based on 'objects', in which data are closely linked to the procedures that operate on them. For example, a circle on the screen might be an object: it has data, such as a centre point and a radius, as well as procedures for moving it, erasing it, changing its size, and so on.

The technique originated with the Simula and Smalltalk languages in the 1960s and early 1970s, but it has since been incorporated into many general-purpose programming languages.

**object program** the ◊machine-code translation of a program written in a ◊source language.

**office automation** introduction of computers and other electronic equipment, such as fax machines, to support an office routine. Increasingly, computers are used to support administrative tasks such as document processing, filing, mail, and schedule management; project planning and management accounting have also been computerized.

**OMR** abbreviation for ◊*optical mark recognition*.

**on-line system** a system that allows the computer to work interactively with its users, responding to each instruction as it is given and prompting users for information when necessary, as opposed to a ◊batch processing system. With the falling cost of computer operation, on-line operation has become increasingly attractive commercially.

**operating system** (OS) a program that controls the basic operation of a computer. A typical OS controls the ◊peripheral devices, organizes the filing system, provides a means of communicating with the operator, and runs other programs.

Some operating systems were written for specific computers, but some are accepted standards. These include CP/M (by Digital Research), widely employed for computers with 8-bit microprocessors; MS-DOS (by Microsoft) for microcomputers with 16-bit microprocessors; and Unix (by Bell Laboratories) for minicomputers.

**operations manager** job classification for ◊computer personnel. An operations manager coordinates all the day-to-day activities of the staff who run the computer applications.

**operator** job classification for ◊computer personnel. A computer operator runs programs.

**optical character recognition** (OCR) a technique for inputting text to a computer by means of a document reader. First, a ◊scanner uses technology similar to that of a photocopier to produce a digital image of the text; then character-recognition software makes use of stored knowledge about the shapes of individual characters to convert the digital image to a set of internal codes that can be stored and processed by computer. OCR is used, for example, by gas and electricity companies to input data collected on meter-reading cards.

At one time OCR required specially designed characters but current devices can recognize most standard typefaces and even handwriting.

**optical computer** computer in which both light and electrical signals are used in the ◊central processing unit. The technology is still not fully developed, but such a computer promises to be faster and less vulnerable to outside electrical interference than one that relies solely on electricity.

**optical disc** a storage medium in which laser technology is used to record and read large volumes of digital data. Types include ◊CD-ROM, ◊WORM, and erasable optical disc.

**optical fibre** very fine, optically pure glass fibre through which light can be reflected to transmit images or data from one end to the other. Optical fibres are increasingly being used to replace metal communications cables, particularly within local area ◊networks, the messages being encoded as digital pulses of light rather than as fluctuating electric current. Although expensive to produce and install, optical fibres can carry more data than traditional cables, and are less susceptible to interference.

**optical mark recognition** (OMR) a technique that enables marks made in predetermined positions on computer-input forms to be detected optically and input into a computer. An *optical mark reader* shines a light beam onto the input document and is able to detect the marks because less light is reflected back from them than from the paler, unmarked paper.

**Oracle** ◊teletext system operated in the UK by Independent Television, introduced in 1973. See also ◊Ceefax.

**OR gate** in electronics, a type of ◊logic gate.

**OS/2** single-user computer ◊operating system produced jointly by Microsoft Corporation and IBM for use on large microcomputers. Its main features are ◊multitasking and the ability to access large amounts of internal ◊memory.

OS/2 was launched 1987, and is partly based on an earlier system, ◊MS-DOS. A second, more powerful version was introduced in 1992.

**output device** any device for displaying, in a form intelligible to the user, the results of processing carried out by a computer.

The most common output devices are the ◊visual display unit (or screen) and the printer. Other output devices include graph plotters, speech synthesizers, and COM (computer output on microfilm/microfiche).

**overflow error** an ◊error that occurs if a number is outside the computer's range and is too large to deal with.

**packet switching** a method of transmitting data between computers connected in a ◊network. A complete packet consists of the data being transmitted and information about which computer is to receive the data. The packet travels around the network until it reaches the correct destination.

**page-description language** control language used to describe the contents and layout of a complete printed page. Page-description languages are frequently used to control the operation of ◊laser printers.

The most popular page-description languages are Adobe Postscript and Hewlett-Packard Printer Control Language.

**page printer** computer ◊printer that prints a complete page of text and graphics at a time. Page printers use electrostatic techniques, very similar to those used by photocopiers, to form images of pages, and range in size from small ◊laser printers designed to work with microcomputers to very large machines designed for high-volume commercial printing.

**paging** method of increasing a computer's apparent memory capacity. See ◊virtual memory.

**parallel device** a device that communicates binary data by sending the bits that represent each character simultaneously along a set of separate data lines, unlike a ◊serial device, which sends data in series along a single data line.

**parallel processing** emerging computer technology that allows more than one computation at the same time. Although in the 1980s this technology enabled only a small number of computer processor units to work in parallel, in theory thousands or millions of processors could be used at the same time. Parallel processing, which involves breaking down computations into small parts and performing thousands of them simultaneously, rather than in a linear sequence, offers the prospect of a vast improvement in working speed for certain repetitive applications.

**parallel running** a method of implementing a new computer system in which the new system and the old system are run together for a short while. The old system is therefore available to take over from its replacement should any faults arise. Compare ◊pilot running.

**parameter** variable factor or characteristic of an object. For example, length is one parameter of a rectangle; its height is another. It is frequently useful to describe a program or object with a set of variable parameters rather than fixed values. For example, if a programmer writes a routine for drawing a rectangle using general parameters for the length, height, line thickness, and so on, any rectangle can be drawn by this routine by giving different values to the parameters.

Similarly, in a word-processing application which contains parameters for font, page layout, type of ◊justification, and so on, these can be changed by the user.

**parity** of a number, the state of being either even or odd. The term refers to the number of 1s in the binary codes used to represent data. A binary representation has *even parity* if it contains an even number of 1s and *odd parity* if it contains an odd number of 1s. For example, the binary code number 1000001, commonly used to represent the character 'A', has even parity because it contains two 1s. By contrast, the binary code 1000011, commonly used to represent the character 'C', has odd parity because it contains three 1s.

A *parity bit* is sometimes added to each binary representation to adjust its parity and enable a ◊validation check to be carried out each time data are transferred from one part of the computer to another. The parity bit is added as either a 1 or a 0 so that, after it has been added, every binary representation has the same parity. So, for example, the codes 1000001 and 1000011 could have parity bits added and become *0*1000001 and *1*1000011, both with even parity. If any bit in these codes should be altered in the course of processing the parity would change and the error would be quickly detected.

**PASCAL** (French acronym for *program appliqué à la selection et la compilation automatique de la litterature*) a high-level programming language. Designed by Niklaus Wirth (1934– ) in the 1960s as an aid to teaching programming, it is still widely used as such in universities, but is also recognized as a good general-purpose programming language. It was named after the 17th-century French mathematician Blaise Pascal.

**password** secret combination of characters used to ensure ◊data security.

**peripheral device** any item of equipment attached to and controlled by a computer. Peripherals are typically for input from and output to the user (for example, a keyboard or printer), storing data (for example, a disc drive), communications (such as a modem), or for performing physical tasks (such as a robot).

**personal computer** (PC) another name for ◊microcomputer. The term is also used, more specifically, to mean the IBM Personal Computer and computers based on it.

The first IBM PC was introduced in 1981; it had 64 kilobytes of random access memory (RAM) and one floppy-disc drive. It was followed in 1983 by the XT (with a hard-disc drive) and in 1984 by the AT (based on a more powerful ◊microprocessor). Many manufacturers have copied the basic design, which is now regarded as a standard for business microcomputers. Computers designed to function like an IBM PC are called ***IBM-compatible computers***.

**pilot running** a method of implementing a new computer system in which the work is gradually transferred from the old system to the new system over a period of time. This ensures that any faults in the new system are resolved before the old system is withdrawn. Compare ◊parallel running.

**PIN** (acronym for *p*ersonal *i*dentification *n*umber) in banking, a unique number used as a password to establish the identity of a customer using an automatic cash dispenser. The PIN is normally encoded into the magnetic strip of the customer's bank card and is known only to the customer and to the bank's computer. Before a cash dispenser will issue money or information, the customer must insert the card into a slot in the machine (so that the PIN can be read from the magnetic strip) and enter the PIN correctly at a keyboard. This prevents stolen cards from being used to obtain money from cash dispensers.

**pixel** (acronym for *pic*ture *el*ement) a single dot on a computer screen. All screen images are made up of a collection of pixels, with each pixel being either off (dark) or on (illuminated, possibly in colour). The number of pixels available determines the screen's resolution. Typical resolutions of microcomputer screens vary from 320 × 200 pixels to 640 × 480 pixels, but screens with over 1,000 × 1,000 pixels are now quite common for high-quality graphic (pictorial) displays.

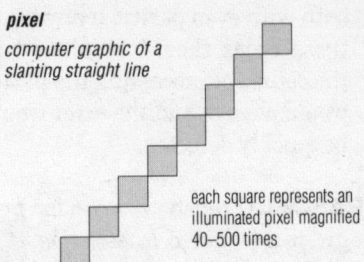

*pixel*
*computer graphic of a slanting straight line*

each square represents an illuminated pixel magnified 40–500 times

The number of bits (binary digits) used to represent each pixel determines how many colours it can display: a two-bit pixel can have four colours; an eight-bit (one-byte) pixel can have 256 colours. The higher the resolution of a screen and the more colours it is capable of displaying, the more memory will be needed to store that screen's contents.

**plotter** or ***graph plotter*** device that draws pictures or diagrams under computer control. Plotters are often used for producing business charts, architectural plans and engineering drawings. ***Flatbed plotters*** move a pen up and down across a flat drawing surface, whereas ***roller plotters*** roll the drawing paper past the pen as it moves from side to side.

**point-of-sale terminal** (POS terminal) computer terminal used in shops to input and output data at

*plotter*

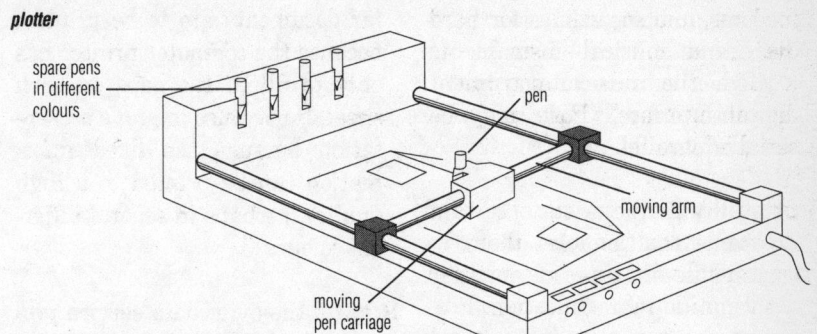

the point where a sale is transacted; for example, at a supermarket checkout. The POS terminal inputs information about the identity of each item sold, retrieves the price and other details from a central computer, and prints out a fully itemized receipt for the customer. It may also input sales data for the shop's computerized stock-control system.

A POS terminal typically has all the facilities of a normal till, including a cash drawer and a sales register, plus facilities for the direct capture of sales information—commonly, a laser scanner for reading bar codes. It may also be equipped with a device to read customers' bank cards, so that payment can be transferred electronically from the customers' bank accounts to the shop's (see ◊EFTPOS).

**polling** a technique for transferring data from a terminal to the central computer of a ◊multiuser system. The computer automatically makes a connection with each terminal in turn, interrogates it to check whether it is holding data for transmission, and, if it is, collects the data.

**port** a socket that enables a computer processor to communicate with an external device. It may be an *input port* (such as a joystick port), or an *output port* (such as a printer port), or both (an *i/o port*).

Microcomputers may provide ports for cartridges, televisions and/or monitors, printers, and modems, and sometimes for hard discs and musical instruments (◊MIDI, the musical-instrument digital interface). Ports may be serial or parallel.

**portability** characteristic of certain programs that enables them to run on different types of computer with minimum modification. Programs written in a ◊high-level language can usually be run on any computer that has a compiler or interpreter for that language.

**portable computer** computer that can be carried from place to place. The term embraces a number of very different computers—from those that would be carried only with some reluctance to those, such as ◊laptop computers and ◊notebook computers, that can be comfortably carried and used in transit.

**preprinted stationery** computer stationery on which certain information has already been printed. Such information might include a company's name and address, or the boxes and lines that make up a form or bill.

Preprinted stationery saves time where large numbers of similar documents are to be printed, because the computer printer has only to fill in the gaps on each sheet. It may also improve presentation because the fixed information can be printed to a high quality, perhaps in several different colours.

**Prestel** the ◊viewdata service provided by British Telecom (BT), which provides information on the television screen via the telephone network. BT pioneered the service in 1975.

**printed circuit board** (PCB) electrical circuit created by laying (printing) 'tracks' of a conductor such as copper on one or both sides of an insulating board. The PCB was invented in 1936 by Austrian scientist Paul Eisler, and was first used on a large scale in 1948.

Components such as integrated circuits (chips), resistors and capacitors can be soldered to the surface of the board (surface-mounted) or, more commonly, attached by inserting their connecting pins or wires into holes drilled in the board. PCBs include ◊motherboards, ◊expansion boards, and adaptors.

*printed circuit board*

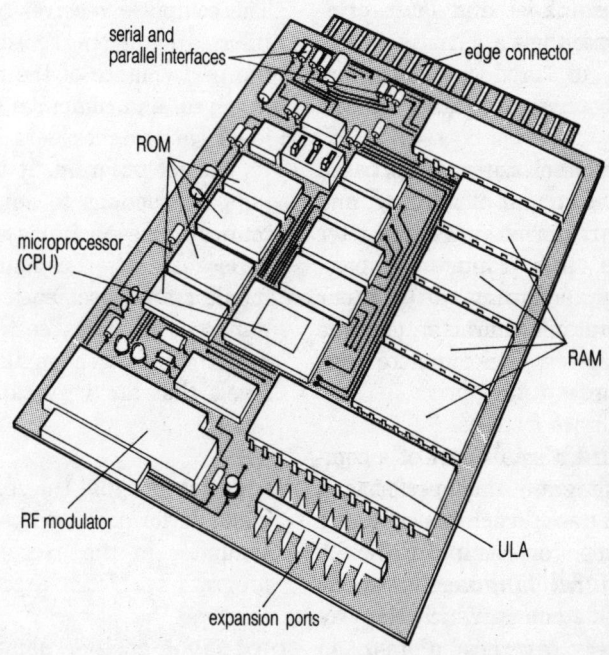

**printer** an output device for producing printed copies of text or graphics. Types include the ◊*daisywheel printer*, which produces good-quality text but no graphics; the ◊*dot-matrix printer*, which produces text and graphics by printing a pattern of small dots; the ◊*ink-jet printer*, which creates text and graphics by spraying a fine jet of quick-drying ink onto the paper; and the ◊*laser printer*, which uses electrostatic technology very similar to that used by a photocopier to produce high-quality text and graphics.

Printers may be classified as *impact printers* (such as daisywheel and dot-matrix printers), which form characters by striking an inked ribbon against the paper, and *non-impact printers* (such as ink-jet and laser printers), which use a variety of techniques to produce characters without physical impact on the paper.

A further classification is based on the basic unit of printing, and categorizes printers as character printers, line printers, or page printers, according to whether they print one character, one line of characters, or a complete page at a time.

**procedure** a small part of a computer program that performs a specific task, such as clearing the screen or sorting a file. A *procedural language*, such as BASIC, is one in which the programmer describes a task in terms of how it is to be done, as opposed to a *declarative language*, such as PROLOG, in which it is described in terms of the required result. See ◊programming. Careful use of procedures is an element of ◊structured programming. In some programming languages there is an overlap between procedures, ◊functions, and ◊subroutines.

**process control** automatic computerized control of a manufacturing process, such as glassmaking. The computer receives ◊feedback information from sensors about the performance of the machines involved, and compares this with ideal performance data stored in its control program. It then outputs instructions to adjust automatically the machines' settings.

Because the computer can monitor and reset each machine hundreds of times each minute, performance can be maintained at levels that are very close to the ideal.

**processing cycle** the sequence of steps performed repeatedly by a computer in the execution of a program; see ◊fetch–execute cycle.

**processor** another name for the ◊central processing unit or ◊microprocessor of a computer.

**program** a set of instructions that controls the operation of a computer. There are two main kinds: ◊applications programs, which carry out tasks for the benefit of the user—for example, word processing; and ◊systems programs, which control the internal workings of the computer. A ▷utility program is a systems program that carries out specific tasks for the user. Programs can be written in any of a number of programming languages but are always translated into machine code before they can be executed by the computer.

**program counter** an alternative name for a ▷sequence-control register.

**program documentation** ▷documentation that provides a complete technical description of a program, built up as the software is written, and is intended to support any later maintenance or development of the program.

**program flow chart** type of ▷flow chart used to describe the flow of data through a particular computer program.

**program loop** a part of a computer program that is repeated several times. The loop may be repeated a fixed number of times (***counter-controlled loop***) or until a certain condition is satisfied (***condition-controlled loop***). For example, a counter-controlled loop might be used to repeat an input routine until exactly ten numbers have been input; a condition-controlled loop might be used to repeat an input routine until the ▷data terminator instruction 'XXX' is entered.

**programmer** job classification for ▷computer personnel. Programmers write the software needed for any new computer system or application.

**programming** writing instructions in a programming language for the control of a computer. ***Applications programming*** is for end-user programs, such as accounts or word-processing packages. ***Systems programming*** is for operating systems and the like, which are concerned more with the internal workings of the computer.

There are several programming styles.

***Procedural programming***, in which programs are written as lists of instructions for the computer to obey in sequence, is by far the most popular. It is the 'natural' style, closely matching the computer's own sequential operation.

*Declarative programming*, as used in the programming language PROLOG, does not describe how to solve a problem, but rather describes its logical structure. Running such a program is more like proving an assertion than following a procedure.

*Functional programming* is a style based largely on the definition of functions. There are very few functional programming languages, HOPE and ML being the most widely used, though many more conventional languages (for example C) make extensive use of functions.

*Object-oriented programming*, the most recently developed style, involves viewing a program as a collection of objects that behave in certain ways when they are passed certain 'messages'. For example, an object might be defined to represent a table of figures, which will be displayed on screen when a 'display' message is received.

**programming language** a special notation in which instructions for controlling a computer are written. Programming languages may be classified as ◊high-level languages or ◊low-level languages. See also ◊source language.

**PROLOG** (acronym for *pro*gramming in *log*ic) high-level programming language based on logic. Invented in 1971 at the University of Marseille, France, it did not achieve widespread use until more than ten years later. It is used mainly for ◊artificial-intelligence programming.

**PROM** (acronym for *p*rogrammable *r*ead-*o*nly *m*emory) a memory device in the form of an integrated circuit (chip) that can be programmed after manufacture to hold information permanently. PROM chips are empty of information when manufactured, unlike ROM (read-only memory) chips, which have information built into them.

Other memory devices are ◊EPROM (erasable programmable read-only memory) and ◊RAM (random-access memory).

**protocol** an agreed set of standards for the transfer of data between different devices. They cover transmission speed, format of data, and the signals required to synchronize the transfer. See also ◊interface.

**pull-down menu** list of options provided as part of a ◊graphical user interface. The presence of pull-down menus is normally indicated by a row of single words at the top of the screen. When the user points at a word with a ◊mouse, a full menu appears (is pulled down) and the user can then select the required option.

In some graphical user interfaces the menus appear from the bottom of the screen and in others they may appear at any point on the screen when a special menu button is pressed on the mouse.

**punched card** an early form of data storage and input, now almost obsolete. The 80-column card widely used in the 1960s and 1970s was a thin card, measuring 190 × 84 mm, holding up to 80 characters of data encoded as small rectangular holes.

The punched card was invented by Joseph-Marie Jacquard (1752–1834) in about 1801 to control weaving looms. The first data-processing machine using punched cards was developed by Herman Hollerith (1860–1929) in the 1880s for the US census.

**RAM** (acronym for *r*andom-*a*ccess *m*emory) a memory device in the form of a collection of integrated circuits (chips), frequently used in microcomputers. Unlike ◊ROM (read-only memory) chips, RAM chips can be both read from and written to by the computer, but their contents are lost when the power is switched off. Microcomputers of the 1990s may have 10–20 megabytes of RAM.

**random access** alternative term for ◊direct access.

**random number** one of a series of numbers having no detectable pattern. Random numbers are used in ◊computer simulation and ◊computer games. It is impossible for an ordinary computer to generate true random numbers, but various techniques are available for obtaining pseudo-random numbers—close enough to true randomness for most purposes.

**range check** a ◊validation check applied to a numerical data item to ensure that its value falls in a sensible range.

**raster graphics** computer graphics that are stored in the computer memory by using a map to record data (such as colour and intensity) for every ◊pixel that makes up the image.

When transformed (enlarged, rotated, stretched, and so on), raster graphics become ragged and suffer loss of picture resolution, unlike ◊vector graphics. Raster graphics are typically used for painting applications, which allow users to create artwork on a computer screen much as if they were painting on paper or canvas.

**real-time system** a program that responds to events in the world as they happen, as, for example, an automatic pilot program in an aircraft must respond instantly in

**record** a collection of related data items or *fields*. A record usually forms part of a ◊file.

**recursion** technique whereby a ◊function or ◊procedure calls itself into use in order to enable a complex problem to be broken down into simpler steps. For example, a function that finds the factorial of a number $n$ (calculates the product of all the whole numbers between 1 and $n$) would obtain its result by multiplying $n$ by the factorial of $n-1$.

**register** a memory location that can be accessed rapidly; it is often built into the computer's central processing unit. Some registers are reserved for special tasks—for example, an *instruction register* is used to hold the machine-code command that the computer is currently executing, while a *sequence-control register* keeps track of the next command to be executed. Other types of register are used for holding frequently used data and for storing intermediate results.

**relational database** ◊database in which data are viewed as a collection of linked tables. It is the most popular of the three basic database models, the others being *network* and *hierarchical*.

**relative** (of a value) variable and calculated from a base value. For example, a *relative address* is a memory location that is found by adding a variable to a base (fixed) address, and a *relative cell reference* locates a cell in a spreadsheet by its position relative to a base cell—perhaps directly to the left of the base cell or three columns to the right of the base cell. The opposite of relative is ◊absolute.

**remote terminal** a terminal that communicates with a computer via a modem (or acoustic coupler) and a telephone line.

**resolution** the number of dots per unit length in which an image can be reproduced on a screen or printer. A typical screen resolution for colour monitors is 75 dpi (dots per inch). A ◊laser printer will typi-

*remote terminal*

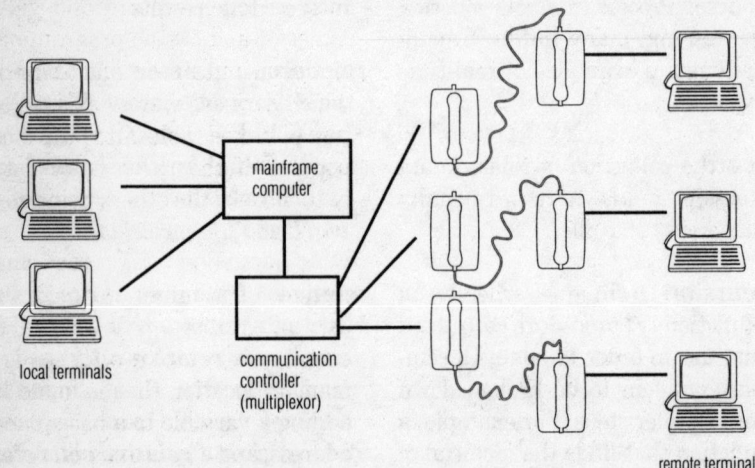

cally have a printing resolution of 300 dpi, and ◊dot-matrix printers typically have resolutions from 60 to 180 dpi. Photographs in books and magazines will have a resolution of 1,200 dpi or 2,400 dpi.

**response time** the delay between entering a command and seeing its effect.

**reverse video** alternative term for ◊*inverse video*.

**RGB** (abbreviation of *red–green–blue*) method of connecting a colour screen to a computer, involving three separate signals: red, green, and blue. All the colours displayed by the screen can be made up from these three component colours.

**RISC** (acronym for *r*educed *i*nstruction-*s*et *c*omputer) microprocessor (processor on a single chip) that carries out fewer instructions than other, ◊CISC, microprocessors in common use in the 1990s. Because of the low number of ◊machine-code instructions, the processor carries out those instructions very quickly.

RISC microprocessors became commercially available in the late 1980s, but are less widespread

*robot*

*robot arm on assembly line*

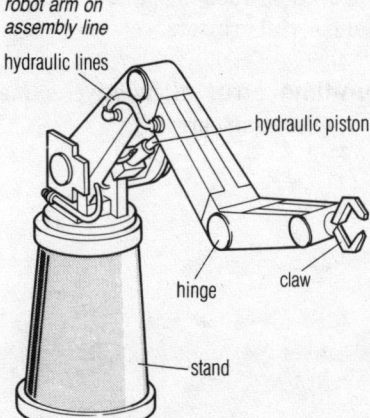

than traditional processors. The Archimedes range of computers, popular in schools, is based on RISC processors.

**robot** any computer-controlled machine that can be programmed to move or carry out work. Robots are often used in industry to transport materials or to perform repetitive tasks. For instance, robotic arms, fixed to a floor or workbench, may be used to paint machine parts or assemble electronic circuits. Other robots are designed to work in situations that would be dangerous to humans—for example, in defusing bombs or in space. Some robots are equipped with sensors, such as touch sensors and video cameras, and can be programmed to make simple decisions based on the sensory data received.

**rogue value** another name for ▷data terminator.

**ROM** (acronym for *r*ead-*o*nly *m*emory) a memory device in the form of a collection of integrated circuits (chips), frequently used in microcomputers. ROM chips are loaded with data and programs during manufacture and, unlike ▷RAM (random-access memory) chips, can subsequently only be read, not written to, by computer. However, the contents of the chips are not lost when the power is switched off, as happens in RAM.

ROM is used to form a computer's permanent store of vital information, or of programs that must be readily available but protected from accidental or deliberate change by a user. For example, of the ▷operating system a microcomputer is often held in ROM memory.

**root directory** top directory in a ▷tree-and-branch filing system. It contains all other directories.

**rounding error** an ◊error that occurs when a decimal result is rounded up or down.

**RS232 interface** standard type of computer ◊interface used to connect computers to serial devices. It is used for modems, mice, screens, and serial printers.

**run-time error** alternative name for execution ◊error.

**scanner** a device that can produce a digital image of a document for input and storage in a computer. It uses technology similar to that of a photocopier. Small scanners can be passed over the document surface by hand; larger versions have a flat bed, resembling that of a photocopier, on which the input document is placed and scanned.

Scanners are widely used to input graphics for use in ▷desktop publishing. If text is input with a scanner, the image captured is seen by the computer as a single digital picture rather than as individual characters. Consequently, the text cannot be processed by, for example, a word processor unless suitable optical character-recognition software is available to convert the image to its constituent characters. Scanners vary in their resolution: hand-held scanners ranging from 75 to 300 dpi (dots per inch).

**screen dump** the process of making a printed copy of the current VDU screen display. The screen dump is sometimes stored as a data file instead of being printed immediately.

**scrolling** the action by which data displayed on a VDU screen are automatically moved upwards and out of sight as new lines of data are added at the bottom.

**searching** extracting a specific item from a large body of data, such as a file or table. The method used depends on how the data are organized. For example, a binary search, which requires the data to be in sequence, involves first deciding which half of the data contains the required item, then which quarter, then which eighth, and so on until the item is found.

**search request** a structured request by a user for information from a ▷database. This may be a simple request for all the entries that have a single field meeting a certain condition. For example, a user searching a file containing car-registration details might request a list of all the records that have 'VAUXHALL' in the ◊field recording the make of car.

In more complex examples, the user may construct a search request using operators like AND, OR, NOT, CONTAINING, and BETWEEN.

An example of a search request using such operators is:

*CAR SEARCH* registration number *containing* XTW *and* make Vauxhall *and* model Astra *and* body hatchback *and* colour blue *or* black *and* registered *between* 1989 *and* 1991

This search request would produce a list of all the black or blue Vauxhall Astra hatchbacks registered between 1989 and 1991 that contained the letters XTW in their registration number.

**sector** part of the magnetic structure created on a disc surface during ◊disc formatting so that data can be stored on it. The disc is first divided into circular tracks and then each circular track is divided into a number of sectors.

**security** protection against loss or misuse of data; see ◊data security.

**semiconductor** a crystalline material with an electrical conductivity between that of metals (good) and insulators (poor).

The conductivity of semiconductors can usually be improved by minute additions of different substances or by other factors. Silicon, for example, has poor conductivity at low temperatures, but this is improved by the application of light, heat, or voltage; hence silicon is used in transistors, rectifiers, and integrated circuits (silicon chips).

**sensor** a device designed to detect a physical state or measure a physical quantity, and produce an input signal for a computer. For example, a sensor may detect the fact that a printer has run out of paper or may measure the temperature in a kiln.

The signal from a sensor is usually in the form of an analogue voltage, and must therefore be converted to a digital signal, by means of an ▷analogue-to-digital converter, before it can be input.

**sequence-control register** or *program counter* a special memory location used to hold the address of the next instruction to be fetched from the immediate-access memory for execution by the computer (see ▷fetch–execute cycle). It is located within the control unit of the ▷central processing unit.

**sequential file** a file in which the records are arranged in order of a ▷key field and the computer can use a searching technique, like a ▷binary search, to access a specific record. See ▷file access.

**serial device** a device that communicates binary data by sending the bits that represent each character one by one along a single data line; a ▷parallel device, by contrast, sends data simultaneously along a number of data lines.

**serial file** a file in which the records are not stored in any particular order and therefore a specific record can be accessed only by reading through all the previous records. See ▷file access.

**silicon chip** ▷integrated circuit with microscopically small electrical components on a piece of silicon crystal only a few millimetres square.

**simulation** short for ▷computer simulation.

**smart card** plastic card with an embedded microprocessor and memory. It can store, for example, personal data, identification, and bank-account details, to enable it to be used as a credit or debit card. The card can be loaded with credits, which are then spent electronically, and are reloaded as needed. Possible other uses range from hotel door 'keys' to passports.

**soft-sectored disc** another name for an unformatted blank disc; see ▷disc formatting.

**software** a collection of programs and procedures for making a computer perform a specific task, as opposed to ▷hardware, the term used to describe the physical components of a computer system. Software is created by programmers and is either distributed on a suitable medium, such as the ◊floppy disc, or built into the computer in the form of ◊firmware. Examples of software include operating systems, compilers, and application programs. No computer can function without some form of software.

**sorting** arranging data in sequence. When sorting a collection, or file, of data made up of several different ◊fields, one must be chosen as the *key field* used to establish the correct sequence. For example, the data in a company's mailing list might include fields for each customer's first names, surname, address, and telephone number. For most purposes the company would wish the records to be sorted alphabetically by surname; therefore, the surname field would be chosen as the key field.

The choice of sorting method involves a compromise between running time, memory usage, and complexity. Those used include *selection sorting*, in which the smallest item is found and exchanged with the first item, the second smallest exchanged with the second item, and so on; *bubble sorting*, in which adjacent items are continually exchanged until the data are in sequence; and *insertion sorting*, in which each item is placed in the correct position and subsequent items moved down to make a place for it.

**source language** the language in which a program is written, as opposed to ◊machine code, which is the form in which the program's instructions are carried out by the computer. Source languages are classified either as ◊high-level languages or as ◊low-level languages, according to whether each notation in the source language stands for many or only one instruction in machine code.

Programs in high-level languages are translated into machine code by either a ◊compiler or an ◊interpreter program. Low-level programs are translated into machine code by means of an ◊assembler program. The program, before translation, is called the *source program*; after translation into machine code it is called the *object program*.

**source program** a program written in a ◊source language.

**speech recognition** or *voice input* any technique by which a computer can understand ordinary speech. Spoken words are divided into 'frames', each lasting about one-thirtieth of a second, which are converted to a wave form. These are then compared with a series of stored frames to determine the most likely word. Research into speech recognition started in 1938, but the technology did not become sufficiently developed for commercial applications until the late 1980s.

There are three types: *separate word recognition* for distinguishing up to several hundred separately spoken words; *connected speech recognition* for speech in which there is a short pause between words; *continuous speech recognition* for normal but carefully articulated speech.

**speech synthesis** or *voice output* computer-based technology for generating speech. A speech synthesizer is controlled by a computer, which supplies strings of codes representing basic speech sounds (phonemes); together these make up words. Speech-synthesis applications include children's toys, car- and aircraft-warning systems, and talking books for the blind.

**spooling** the process in which information to be printed is stored temporarily in a file, the printing being carried out later. It is used to prevent a relatively slow printer from holding up the system at critical times, and to enable several computers or programs to share one printer.

**spreadsheet** a program that mimics a sheet of ruled paper, divided into columns and rows. The user enters values in the sheet, then instructs the program to perform some operation on them, such as totalling a column or finding the average of a series of numbers. Highly complex numerical analyses may be built up from these simple steps.

Spreadsheets are widely used in business for forecasting and financial control. The first spreadsheet program, VisiCalc, appeared in 1979. The best known include Lotus 1–2–3 and Excel.

**sprite** a graphics object made up of a pattern of ◊pixels (picture elements) defined by a computer

*spreadsheet*

| | A | B | C | D | E |
|---|---|---|---|---|---|
| | COMPUTER SUPPLIES ORDER (SS) | | | | |
| 1 | DESCRIPTION | | NUMBER | UNIT COST(£) | COST |
| 2 | | | | | |
| 3 | FLOPPY DISCS | | 50 | 0.55 | 27.5 |
| 4 | INK RIBBONS | | 10 | 2.25 | 22.5 |
| 5 | INK JET CARTRIDGES | | 5 | 12.5 | 62.5 |
| 6 | PAPER (BOX 500 SHEETS) | | 12 | 3.75 | 45 |
| 7 | | | | | |
| 8 | | | | TOTAL COST | £ 157.50 |
| 9 | | | | | |
| 10 | | | | | |

programmer. Some ◊high-level languages and ◊applications programs contain routines that allow a user to define the shape, colours, and other characteristics of individual graphics objects. These objects can then be manipulated to produce animated games or graphic screen displays.

**SQL** (abbreviation of ***structured query language***) high-level programming language designed for use with ◊relational databases. Although it can be used by programmers in the same way as other languages, it is often used as a means for programs to communicate with each other. Typically, one program (called the 'client') uses SQL to request data from a database 'server'.

**SRAM** (acronym for *s*tatic *r*andom-*a*ccess *m*emory) computer memory device in the form of a silicon chip that is used to provide immediate-access memory. SRAM is faster but more expensive than ◊DRAM (dynamic random-access memory).

DRAM loses its contents unless they are read and rewritten every 2 milliseconds or so. This process is called *refreshing* the memory. SRAM does not require such frequent refreshing.

**stack** a method of storing data in which the most recent item stored will be the first to be retrieved. The technique is commonly called 'last in, first out'.

Stacks are used to solve problems involving nested structures; for example, to analyse an arithmetical expression that contains subexpressions in parentheses, or to work out a route between two points when there are many different paths.

**stand-alone computer** self-contained computer, usually a microcomputer, that is not connected to a network of computers and can be used in isolation from any other device.

**stepper motor** electric motor that can be precisely controlled by signals from a computer. The motor turns through a precise angle each time it receives a signal pulse from the computer. By varying the rate at which signal pulses are produced, the motor can be run at different speeds or turned through an exact angle and then stopped. Switching circuits can be constructed to allow the computer to reverse the motor's direction.

By combining two or more motors, complex movement control becomes possible. For example, if stepper motors are used to power the wheels of a small vehicle a computer can manoeuver the vehicle in any direction.

Stepper motors are commonly used in small-scale applications where computer-controlled movement is required, for example in disc drives. In larger applications, where greater power is necessary, pneumatic or hydraulic systems are usually preferred.

**string** group of characters manipulated as a single object by the computer. In its simplest form a string may consist of a single letter or word—for example, the single word SMITH might be established as a string for processing by a computer. A string can also consist of a combination of words, spaces, and numbers—for example, 33 HIGH STREET ANYTOWN ALLSHIRE could be established as a single string.

Most high-level languages have a variety of string-handling ◊functions. For example, functions may be provided to read a character from any given position in a string or to count automatically the number of characters present in a string.

**structured programming** the process of writing a program in small, independent parts. This makes it easier to control a program's development and to design and test its individual component parts. Structured programs are built up from units called ***modules***, which normally correspond to single ◊procedures or ◊functions. Some programming languages, such as PASCAL and Modula-2, are better suited to structured programming than others.

**subroutine** a small section of a program that is executed ('called') from another part of the program. Subroutines provide a method of performing the same task at more than one point in the program, and also of separating the details of a program from its main logic. In some computer languages, subroutines are similar to ◊functions or ◊procedures.

**supercomputer** the fastest, most powerful type of computer available. It is capable of performing its basic operations in picoseconds (thousand-billionths of a second), rather than nanoseconds (billionths of a second), like most other computers.

To achieve these extraordinary speeds, supercomputers make use of several processors working together, and techniques such as cooling processors down to temperatures approaching absolute zero (−273°C), so that their components conduct electricity many times faster than normal. Supercomputers are used in weather forecasting, fluid dynamics and aerodynamics. Manufacturers include Cray.

**support environment** a collection of programs (◊software) used to help people design and write other programs. At its simplest, this includes a ◊text editor (word-processing software) and a ◊compiler for translating programs into executable form; but it can also include interactive debuggers for helping to locate faults, data dictionaries for keeping track of the data used, and rapid prototyping tools for producing quick, experimental mock-ups of programs.

**symbolic address** a symbol used in ◊assembly-language programming to represent the binary ◊address of a memory location.

**syntax error** ◊error caused by incorrect use of the programming language.

**system flow chart** type of ◊flow chart used to describe the flow of data through a particular computer system.

**system implementation** the process of installing a new computer system.

To ensure that a system's implementation takes place as efficiently and with as little disruption as possible, a number of tasks are necessary. These include ordering and installing new equipment, ordering new stationery and storage media, training personnel, converting data files into new formats, drawing up an overall implementation plan, and preparing for a period of either ◊parallel running or ◊pilot running.

**systems analysis** the investigation of a business activity or clerical procedure, with a view to deciding if and how it can be computerized. The analyst discusses the existing procedures with the people involved, observes the flow of data through the business, and draws up an outline specification of the required computer system (see also ◊systems design).

Systems in use in the 1990s include Yourdon, SSADM, and Soft Systems Methodology.

**systems analyst** person who carries out systems analysis; see also ◊computer personnel.

**systems design** the detailed design of an ◊applications package. The designer breaks the system down into component programs, and designs the required input forms, screen layouts, and printouts. Systems design forms a link between systems analysis and ◊programming.

**systems program** a program that performs a task related to the operation and performance of the computer system itself. For example, a systems program might control the operation of the display screen, or control and organize backing storage. In contrast, an ◊applications program is designed to carry out tasks for the benefit of the computer user.

**System X** in communications, a modular, computer-controlled,

## System X

digital switching system employed in telephone exchanges. System X was originally developed by the UK companies GEC, Plessey, and STC at the request of the Post Office, beginning in 1969. A prototype exchange was finally commissioned in 1978, and the system launched in 1980.

**tape streamer** a backing storage device consisting of a continuous loop of magnetic tape. Tape streamers are largely used to store dumps (rapid backup copies) of important data files (see ◊data security).

**teletext** broadcast system whereby information is displayed on a television screen. The information—typically about news items, entertainment, sport, and finance—is constantly updated. Teletext is a form of ◊videotext, pioneered in Britain by the British Broadcasting Corporation (BBC) with Ceefax and by Independent Television with Oracle.

**terminal** a device consisting of a keyboard and display screen (◊visual display unit)—or, in older systems, a teleprinter—to enable the operator to communicate with the computer. The terminal may be physically attached to the computer or linked to it by a telephone line (remote terminal). A ***dumb terminal*** has no processor of its own, whereas an ***intelligent terminal*** has its own processor and takes some of the processing load away from the main computer.

**test data** data designed to test whether a new computer program is functioning correctly. The test data are carefully chosen to ensure that all possible branches of the program are tested. The expected results of running the data are written down and are then compared with the actual results obtained by using the program.

**text editor** a program that allows the user to edit text on the screen and to store it in a file. Text editors are similar to ◊word processors, except that they lack the ability to format text into para-

*teletext*

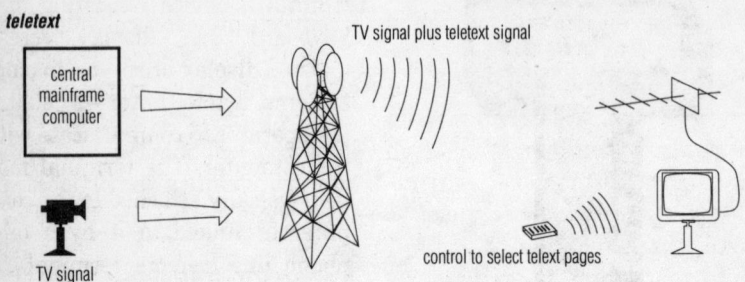

graphs and pages and to apply different typefaces and styles.

**time-sharing** a way of enabling several users to access the same computer at the same time. The computer can rapidly switch between user ◊terminals and programs, allowing each user to work as if he or she had sole use of the system.

Time-sharing was common in the 1960s and 1970s before the spread of cheaper computers.

**topology** in computing, the arrangement of devices in a ◊network.

**touch screen** an input device allowing the user to communicate with the computer by touching a display screen with a finger. In this way, the user can point to a required ◊menu option or item of data. Touch screens are used less than other pointing devices such as the mouse or joystick.

Typically, the screen is able to detect the touch either because the finger presses against a sensitive membrane or because it interrupts a grid of light beams crossing the screen surface.

**touch sensor** in a computer-controlled ◊robot, a device used to give the robot a sense of touch, allowing it to manipulate delicate objects or move automatically about a room. Touch sensors provide the feedback necessary for the robot to adjust the force of its movements and the pressure of its grip. The main types include the strain gauge and the microswitch.

**trace** a method of checking that a computer program is functioning correctly by causing the changing values of all of the ◊variables involved to be displayed while the program is running. In this way it becomes possible to narrow down the search for a bug, or error, in the program to the exact instruction that causes the variables to take unexpected values.

Extra program instructions may have to be inserted to produce a trace, or a ◊utility program may be used to generate a trace automatically when the program is run.

**track** part of the magnetic structure created on a disc surface during ◊disc formatting so that data can be stored on it. The disc is first divided into circular tracks and then each circular track is divided into a number of sectors.

**transaction file** a file that contains all the additions, deletions, and amendments required during ◊file updating to produce a new version of a master file.

**transducer** device that converts one form of energy into another. For example, a thermistor is a transducer that converts heat into an electrical voltage, and an electric motor is a transducer that converts an electrical voltage into mechanical energy. Transducers are important components in many types of ◊sensor, converting the physical quantity that is to be measured into a proportional voltage signal.

**transistor–transistor logic** (TTL) the type of integrated circuit most commonly used in building electronic products. In TTL chips the bipolar transistors are directly connected (usually collector to base). In mass-produced items, large numbers of TTL chips are commonly replaced by a small number of ◊uncommitted logic arrays, or logic gate arrays.

**translation program** a program that translates another program written in a high-level language or assembly language into the machine-code instructions that a computer can obey. See also ◊assembler, ◊compiler, and ◊interpreter.

**transputer** a member of a family of microprocessors designed for parallel processing, developed in the UK by Inmos. In the circuits of a standard computer the processing of data takes place in sequence; in

*tree-and-branch filing system*

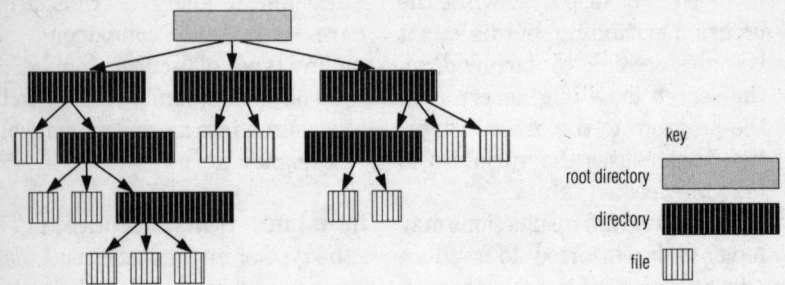

a transputer's circuits processing takes place in parallel, greatly reducing computing time for programs specifically written for it.

The transputer implements a special programming language called Occam, which Inmos based on CSP (communicating sequential processes), developed by C A R Hoare of Oxford University Computing Laboratory.

**tree-and-branch filing system** a filing system where all files are stored within directories, like folders in a filing cabinet. These directories may in turn be stored within further directories. The root directory contains all the other directories and may be thought of as equivalent to the filing cabinet. Another way of picturing the system is as a tree with branches from which grow smaller branches, ending in leaves (individual files).

**Trojan horse** a ◊virus program that appears to function normally but, while undetected by the normal user, causes damage to other files or circumvents security procedures. The earliest appeared in the UK in about 1988.

**truncation error** an ◊error that occurs when a decimal result is cut off (truncated) after the maximum number of places allowed by the computer's level of accuracy.

**truth table** in electronics, a diagram that shows the effect of a particular ◊logic gate on every combination of inputs.

Every possible combination of inputs and outputs for a particular gate or combination of gates is described, thereby defining their action in full. When logic value 1 is written in the table, it indicates a 'high' (or 'yes') input of perhaps 5 volts; logic value 0 indicates a 'low' (or 'no') input of 0 volts.

**TTL** abbreviation for ◊*transistor–transistor logic*, a family of integrated circuits.

**turnaround document** output document produced by a computer that is later, after additional data have been added, used as an input document.

For example, the meter-reading cards produced by gas and electricity companies are a form of turnaround document. Each card is output with customer details printed in a typeface readable by OCR (optical character recognition) and with a standard grid suitable for OMR (optical mark recognition). The meter reader inspects the customer's meter, marks the new reading on the grid, and then returns the card to the company's billing department. There, a *universal document reader*, capable of reading both OCR and OMR data, is used to input the new information to the computer.

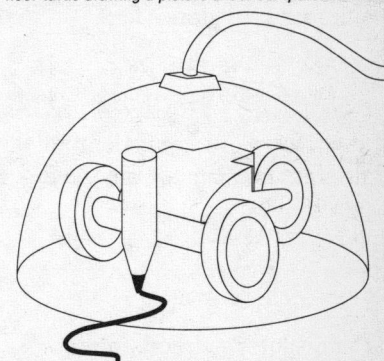

*turtle*
floor turtle drawing a picture under computer control

**turtle** small computer-controlled wheeled robot. The turtle's movements are determined by programs written by a computer user, typically using the programming language ◊LOGO.

**two's complement number system** number system, based on the ◊binary number system, that allows both positive and negative numbers to be conveniently represented for manipulation by a computer.

In the two's complement system the most significant column heading (the furthest to the left) is always taken to represent a negative number. For example, the

## two's complement number system

four-column two's complement number 1101 stands for:

| $-8s$ | $4s$ | $2s$ | $1s$ |
|---|---|---|---|
| 1 | 1 | 0 | 1 |

It is therefore equivalent to the decimal number $-3$, since $-8 + 4 + 1 = -3$.

**ULA** abbreviation for ⟡*uncommitted logic array*.

**uncommitted logic array** (ULA) or *gate array* a type of semicustomized integrated circuit in which the logic gates are laid down to a general-purpose design but are not connected to each other. The interconnections can then be set in place according to the requirements of individual manufacturers. Producing ULAs may be cheaper than using a large number of TTL (⟡transistor–transistor logic) chips or commissioning a fully customized chip.

**underflow error** an ⟡error that occurs if a number is outside the computer's range and is too small to deal with.

**Unix** multiuser ⟡operating system designed for minicomputers but increasingly popular on larger microcomputers, workstations, and supercomputers.

It was developed by Bell Laboratories in the USA during the late 1960s, using the programming language ⟡C. It could therefore run on any machine with a C compiler, so ensuring its wide portability. Its wide range of functions and flexibility have made it widely used by universities and in commercial software.

**user documentation** ⟡documentation that is provided to explain how to operate software.

**user ID** (contraction of *user id*entification) alternative name for ⟡password.

**user interface** the procedures and methods through which the user operates a program. These might include ⟡menus, input forms, error messages, and keyboard procedures. A ⟡graphical user interface (GUI or WIMP) is one that makes use of icons (small pictures) and allows the user to make menu selections with a mouse.

The study of the ways in which people interact with computers is a subbranch of ergonomics. It aims to make it easier for people to use computers effectively and comfortably, and has become a focus of research for many national and international programmes.

**utility program** a systems program designed to perform a specific task related to the operation of the computer when requested to do so by the computer user. For example, a utility program might be used to complete a screen dump, format a disc, or convert the format of a data file so that it can be accessed by a different applications program.

**validation** the process of checking input data to ensure that they are complete, accurate, and reasonable. Although it would be impossible to guarantee that only valid data are entered into a computer, a suitable combination of validation checks should ensure that most errors are detected.

Common validation checks include:

*character-type check* Each input data item is checked to ensure that it does not contain invalid characters. For example, an input name might be checked to ensure that it contains only letters of the alphabet, or an input six-figure date might be checked to ensure that it contains only numbers.

*field-length check* The number of characters in an input field is checked to ensure that the correct number of characters has been entered. For example, a six-figure date field might be checked to ensure that it does contain exactly six digits.

*control-total check* The arithmetic total of a specific field from a group of records is calculated—for example, the hours worked by a group of employees might be added together—and then input with the data to which it refers. The program recalculates the control total and compares it with the one entered to ensure that entry errors have not been made.

*hash-total check* An otherwise meaningless control total is calculated—for example, by adding together account numbers. Even though the total has no arithmetic meaning, it can still be used to check the validity of the input account numbers.

*parity check* Parity bits are added to binary number codes to ensure that each number in a set of data has the same ◊parity (that each binary number has an even number of 1s, for example). The binary numbers can then be checked to ensure that their parity remains the same. This check is often applied to data after it has been transferred from one part of the computer to another; for example, from a disc drive into the immediate-access memory.

*check digit* A digit is calculated from the digits of a code number and then added to that number as an extra digit. For example, in the ISBN (International Standard Book Number) 0 631 90057 8, the 8 is a check digit calculated from the book code number 063190057 and then added to it to make the full ISBN. When the full code number is input, the computer recalculates the check digit and compares it with the one entered. If the entered and calculated check digits do not match, the computer reports that an entry error of some kind has been made.

*range check* An input numerical data item is checked to ensure that its value falls in a sensible range. For example, an input two-digit day of the month might be checked to ensure that it is in the range 01 to 31.

**variable** quantity that can take different values. Variables play an important role in computer programming because they can be used to represent different items of data in the course of a program.

A computer programmer will choose a symbol to represent each variable used in a program. The computer will then automatically assign a memory location to store the current value of each variable, and use the chosen symbol as a means of identifying this location. For example, the letter $P$ might be chosen by a programmer to represent the price of an article. The computer would automatically reserve a memory location with the symbolic address $P$ to store the price being currently processed.

Different programming languages place different restrictions on the choice of symbols used to represent variables. Some languages only allow a single letter followed, where required, by a single number. Other languages allow a much freer choice, allowing, for example, the use of the full word 'price' to represent the price of an article.

A *global variable* is one that can be accessed by any program instruction; a *local variable* is one that can only be accessed by the instructions within a particular subroutine.

**VDU** abbreviation for ◊visual display unit.

**vector graphics** computer graphics that are stored in the computer memory by using geometric formulas. Vector graphics can be transformed (enlarged, rotated, stretched, and so on) without loss of picture resolution. It is also possible to select and transform any of the components of a vector-graphics display because each is separately defined in the computer memory. In these respects vector graphics are superior to ◊raster graphics.

Vector graphics are typically used for drawing applications, allowing the user to create and modify technical diagrams like designs for houses or cars.

**verification** the process of checking that data being input to a computer have been accurately copied from a source document. This may be done visually, by checking the original copy of the data against the copy shown on the VDU screen. A more thorough method is to enter the data twice, using two different keyboard operators, and then to check the two sets of input copies against each other. The checking is normally carried out by the computer itself, any differences between the two copies being reported for correction by one of the keyboard operators.

Where large quantities of data have to be input, a separate machine called a *verifier* may be used to prepare fully verified tapes or discs for direct input to the main computer.

**videotext** system in which information (text and simple pictures) is displayed on a television (video) screen. There are two basic systems, known as ◊teletext and ◊viewdata. In the teletext system information is broadcast with the ordinary television signals, whereas in the viewdata system information is relayed to the screen from a central data bank via the telephone network. Both systems require the use of a television receiver with a special decoder.

**viewdata** system of displaying information on a television screen in which the information is extracted from a computer data bank and transmitted via the telephone lines. It is one form of

◊videotext. The British Post Office (now British Telecom) developed the world's first viewdata system, Prestel, in 1975, and similar systems are now in widespread use in other countries. Viewdata users have access to an almost unlimited store of information, presented on the screen in the form of 'pages'.

Prestel has hundreds of thousands of pages, presenting all kinds of information, from local weather and restaurant menus to share prices and airport timetables. Since viewdata employs telephone lines, it can become a two-way interactive information system, making possible, for example, home banking and shopping. In contrast, the only user input allowed by the ◊teletext system is to select the information to be displayed.

**virtual** without physical existence. Some computers have virtual memory, making their immediate-access memory seem larger than it is; some computers can also simulate *virtual devices*—for example, the Acorn A3000 and A5000 computers have only one floppy-disc drive but can behave as if they were equipped with two, using part of the ◊RAM to simulate the second drive. ◊Virtual reality is a computer simulation of a whole physical environment.

**virtual memory** a technique whereby a portion of the computer backing storage, or external, ◊memory is used as an extension of its immediate-access, or internal, memory. The contents of an area of the immediate-access memory are stored on, say, a hard disc while they are not needed, and brought back into main memory when required.

The process, called paging or segmentation, is controlled by the computer ◊operating system and is hidden from the programmer, to whom the computer's internal memory appears larger than it really is. The technique can be successfully implemented only if very fast backing store is available, so that 'pages' of memory can be rapidly switched into and out of the immediate-access memory.

**virtual reality** advanced form of computer simulation, in which a participant has the illusion of being part of an artificial environment. The participant views the environment through two three-dimensional television screens built into a visor. Sensors detect movements of the head or body, causing the apparent viewing position to change. Gloves (datagloves) fitted with sensors may be worn, which allow the participant seemingly to pick up and move objects in the environment. The technology is still under development but is expected to have widespread applications; for example, in military and surgical training, architecture, and home entertainment.

**virus** a piece of ◊software that can replicate itself and transfer itself from one computer to another, without the user being aware of it. Some viruses are relatively harmless, but others can damage or destroy data. They are written by anonymous programmers, often maliciously, and are spread along telephone lines or on ◊floppy discs. Antivirus software can be used to detect and destroy well-known viruses, but new viruses continually appear and these may bypass existing antivirus programs.

**vision system** computer-based device used to interpret visual signals from a video camera. Computer vision is important in robotics where sensory abilities would greatly increase the flexibility and usefulness of a robot.

Although some vision systems exist for recognizing simple shapes, the technology is still in its infancy.

**visual display unit** (VDU) computer terminal consisting of a keyboard for inputting data and a screen for displaying output. The oldest and the most popular type of VDU screen is the cathode-ray tube (CRT), which uses essentially the same technology as a television screen. Other types use plasma display technology and ◊liquid-crystal displays.

**VLSI** (abbreviation for *very large-scale integration*) in electronics, the early-1990s level of advanced technology to be found in the microminiaturization of ◊integrated circuits, and an order of magnitude smaller than ◊LSI (large-scale integration).

**voice input** alternative name for ◊speech recognition.

**voice output** alternative name for ◊speech synthesis.

**volatile memory** ▷memory that will lose its contents when the power supply to the computer is disconnected.

**WAN** acronym for ◊wide area network.

**wide area network** a ◊network that connects computers over a wide geographical area.

**WIMP** (acronym for *w*indows, *i*cons, *m*enus, *p*ointing device) another name for ◊graphical user interface (GUI).

**Winchester drive** a small hard-disc drive commonly used with microcomputers; *Winchester disc* has become synonymous with ◊hard disc.

**window** rectangular area on the screen of a ◊graphical user interface. A window is used to display data and can be manipulated in various ways by the computer user.

**word** a group of bits (binary digits) that a computer's central processing unit treats as a single working unit. The size of a word varies from one computer to another and, in general, increasing the word length leads to a faster and more powerful computer.

In the late 1970s and early 1980s, most microcomputers were 8-bit machines. During the 1980s 16-bit microcomputers were introduced and 32-bit microcomputers are now available. Mainframe computers may be 32-bit or 64-bit machines.

**word processor** a program that allows for the input, amendment, manipulation, storage, and retrieval of text; or a computer system that runs such software. Since word-processing programs became available for microcomputers, the method has been gradually replacing the typewriter for producing letters or other text.

Typical facilities include insert, delete, cut and paste, reformat, search and replace, copy, print, mail merge, and spelling check.

**WORM** (acronym for *w*rite *o*nce *r*ead *m*any times) a storage device, similar to ▷CD-ROM. The computer can write to the disc directly, but cannot later erase or overwrite the same area. WORMs are mainly used for archiving and backup copies.

**write protection** device on discs and tapes that provides ▷data security by allowing data to be read but not deleted, altered, or overwritten.

**WYSIWYG** (acronym for *w*hat *y*ou *s*ee *i*s *w*hat *y*ou *g*et) a program that attempts to display on the screen a faithful representation of the final printed output. For example, a WYSIWYG ▷word processor would show actual line widths, page breaks, and the sizes and styles of type.

# APPENDIX

## Thematic list of computing terms

### *computer architecture*

- access
- access time
- accumulator
- adder
- address
- address bus
- ALU
- analogue computer
- AND gate
- arithmetic and logic unit
- backup system
- bistable circuit
- buffer
- bus
- cache memory
- central processing unit
- Centronics interface
- chip
- CISC
- clock interrupt
- clock rate
- CMOS
- complementary metal-oxide semiconductor
- computer
- computer generation
- computer history
- control bus
- control unit
- CPU
- data bus
- decoder
- dedicated computer
- digital computer
- DRAM
- edge connector
- EEPROM
- fetch-execute cycle
- fifth-generation computer
- firmware
- flag
- flash memory
- flip-flop
- front-end processor
- function key
- gate
- gigabyte
- hardware
- hertz
- immediate-access memory
- instruction register
- integrated circuit
- interface
- interrupt
- laptop computer
- logic gate
- LSI
- Macintosh
- mainframe
- microchip

# Appendix

microcomputer
microprocessor
MIDI
minicomputer
MIPS
motherboard
multiuser
multitasking
NAND gate
NOR gate
NOT gate
notebook computer
optical computer
OR gate
parallel computing
peripheral device
personal computer
portable computer
printed circuit board
processing cycle
processor
program counter
PROM
real-time system
register
RISC
RS232 interface
semiconductor
sequence-control register
silicon chip
smart card
SRAM
stand alone
supercomputer
time sharing

transistor–transistor logic
transputer
truth table
TTL
ULA
uncommitted logic array
VLSI

## *computer control*

ADC
analogue-to-digital converter
DAC
data logging
digital-to-analogue converter
feedback (open-loop, closed-loop)
flight simulator
sensor
stepper motor
touch sensor
transducer
turtle
vision system

## *communications*

acoustic coupler
baud
Ceefax
Centronics interface
data communications
digital data transmission
encryption

fax
fibre optics
handshake
hertz
integrated services digital network
interface
local area network
MIDI
modem
multiplexer
network
Oracle
packet switching
parallel device
polling
port
protocol
serial device
System X
teletext
videotext
viewdata
wide area network

***data processing***

batch processing
binary search
bureau
character-type check
check digit
computer engineer
computer personnel
control total

data capture
data control staff
data-flow chart
data input
data preparation
data-preparation staff
data processing
data-processing manager
data protection
data security
direct access
direct data entry
document
documentation
dump
EFTPOS
electronic mail
field
field-length check
file
file access
file generations
file librarian
file merging
file searching
file sorting
file transfer
file updating
file protection
GIGO
grandfather-father-son system
hash total
indexed sequential file
ISBN
justification

# Appendix

key
key-to-disc or key-to-tape system
Kimball tag
logical error
master file
media
media librarian
office automation
on-line system
operations manager
operator
parity check
password
PIN
preprinted stationery
random-access file
range check
record
searching
sequential-access file
serial-access file
sorting
transaction file
turnaround document
user ID
validation
verification

## *data representation*

acronym
alphanumeric data
analogue
ASCII
binary number code
binary number system
bit
block
byte
character
character set
corruption of data
data
digit
digital
EBCDIC
fixed-point arithmetic
floating-point arithmetic
hexadecimal number system
instruction set
kilobyte
megabyte
octal number system
parity
two's complement number system
word

## *data storage*

access
access time
backing storage
bubble memory
cache memory
CD-ROM
DAT
data compression
digital audio tape

# Appendix

directory
disc
disc drive
disc formatting
EEPROM
EPROM
field
file
flash memory
floppy disc
gigabyte
hard disc
hard sectored disc
immediate-access memory
inverted file
kilobyte
magnetic tape
mass storage system
media
megabyte
memory
non-volatile memory
paging
punched card
RAM
ROM
root directory
search request
sector
tape streamer
track
volatile memory
Winchester disc
WORM
write protection

## *interactive computing*

computer terminal
hacking
icon
intelligent terminal
interactive computing
interactive video
log off
log on
mouse
POS terminal
pull-down menu
Prestel
remote terminal
response time
terminal
touch screen
VDU
visual display unit
WIMP
window

## *input devices*

bar code
digitizer
document reader
graphical user interface
graphics tablet
GUI
input device
joystick
keyboard

# Appendix

light pen
magnetic strip (stripe)
mark sensing
menu
MICR
mouse
OCR
OMR
pull-down memory
scanner
speech recognition
user interface
voice input

## *output devices*

character printer
COM
computer output on microfilm
daisywheel
dot-matrix printer
fount
graph plotter
hard copy
impact printer
ink-jet printer
inverse video
laser printer
light-emitting diode
line printer
liquid-crystal display
microfiche
microform
output device
page-description language
page printer
pixel
plotter
printer
raster graphics
resolution
RGB
screen dump
scroll
speech synthesis
spooling
vector graphics
voice output

## *programming*

absolute
algorithm
argument
array
benchmark
bubble sort
bug
data terminator
debugging
decision table
driver
dry running
error
error message
execution error
flow chart (program system)
function

global variable
heuristics
interrupt
iteration
jump
library program
local variable
macro
object-oriented programming
overflow error
parameter
procedure
program
program documentation
program flow chart
program loop
programmer
programming
random number
recursion
relative
rogue value
rounding error
run-time error
sprite
stack
string
structured programming
subroutine
symbolic address
syntax error
systems program
test data
trace
truncation error

underflow error
user documentation
variable
virtual
virtual memory

## *programming languages*

ADA
ALGOL
assembler
assembly language
BASIC
C
COBOL
command language
compiler
FORTRAN
fourth-generation language
high-level language
interpreter
LISP
LOGO
low-level language
machine code
mnemonic
object program
PASCAL
portability
programming language
PROLOG
source language
source program

# Appendix

SQL
translation program

## systems analysis

analyst
feasibility study
parallel running
pilot running
system flow chart
system implementation
systems analysis
systems analyst
systems design

## software and applications

application package
application programme
artificial intelligence
boot
bug
CAD
CAL
CAM
CAT scan
CNC
computer-aided design
computer-aided manufacture
computer-assisted learning
computer game
computer graphics
computer numerical control
computer simulation
CP/M
critical-path analysis
cursor
database
dBASE
desktop publishing
DOS
emulator
expert system
export file
Hypertext
import file
knowledge-based system
Lotus 1–2–3
mail merge
MS-DOS
multimedia
operating system
OS-2
process control
relational database
search request
simulation
software
spreadsheet
text editor
Trojan horse
Unix
utility programme
virtual reality
virus
word processor